Job 10:1 "I loathe my very life;
   therefore I will give free rein to my complaint
   and speak out in the bitterness of my soul."

"There's a time when the operation of the machine becomes so odious, makes you so sick at heart, that you can't take part, you can't even passively take part, and you've got to put your bodies on the gears and upon the wheels, upon the levers, upon all the apparatus, and you've got to make it stop!"
—*Mario Savio*

"Sausage is a little bit like life; you get out of it what you put into it."
—*Jimmy Dean*

SuiPsalms

John Edward
LAWSON

I sacrifice this collection in the name of Ixtab and Ab Kin Xoc

Acknowledgements

"A Brief History of Mummies" first published in *The Dream People*
"Chick Magnet" and "Perverted Uncle On Park Bench" first published in *Doorways Magazine*
"A Death Less Ordinary" first published in the *Anthology 2011* program

SuiPsalms © 2012
by John Edward Lawson

Published by Raw Dog Screaming Press
Bowie, MD

All rights reserved.

First Edition

Cover design and illustration: Jennifer C. Barnes
Book design: M. Garrow Bourke

ISBN 978-1-935738-06-0

LCCN 2012900487

Printed in the United States of America

www.RawDogScreaming.com

Also by John Edward Lawson

Novels
New Mosque City
Last Burn in Hell: Director's Cut

Collections
Lawson vs. LaValley (w/Dustin LaValley)
Discouraging at Best
Pocket Full of Loose Razorblades

Poetry
The Troublesome Amputee
The Plague Factory

Illustrated Books
A Child's Guide to Death
(w/Darin Malfi, Dustin LaValley, and Mark Sullivan)

As Editor
Tempting Disaster
Sick
Of Flesh and Hunger

Author's Note

IN MY EXPERIENCE there exists no four-letter word vulgar enough to encompass the profanity of this world, the insult that is consciousness…so I offer instead this book.

Call it career suicide. Editors will be appalled at the notion that authors could expect publishers to unleash this variety of text. Critics will feel their spines melt at having to analyze the work on their own, without assistance from back cover tripe or summaries in the PR kit. This is certainly no help, as author's notes go, since they are typically meant to explain "artistic intent."

Well, here's my intent: a fist in your eye. If that does not appeal to your notions of leisure or the pursuit of self-improvement via "the readerly experience" I suggest you do read this book, because it will hurt you all the more.

As with most authors hoping to impress an air of loftiness upon readers you will find quotes scattered throughout this book. They are intended to dupe you into suspecting there is something "thought-provoking" between these covers.

Don't blame me; our system of higher education attacks any who seek to publish original thoughts. Everything coming out of the academic world has been hashed and rehashed for a hundred years because the professors and grad students can use the originators of the ideas as shields. And the universities wonder why students think it's okay to download term papers and pass them off as their own work?

It's no different in the private sector. Behind closed doors the editors at major publishing houses will confide in you the crux of their belief system: they are not in the business of funding art, they are in the business of gratifying the readership. Meaning your plot, characters, and ending must be hackneyed to the point that those without high school diplomas should be able to fill in the details well in advance. Then, when the utterly predictable occurs, the reader "feels smart." They buy more books of the same caliber in order to revel in the sensation of an inflated IQ/ego.

Bearing that in mind, after this manuscript goes to press you will be able to find my body exactly where you envision, in the condition you suspicioned. And, yes, I will have terminated myself in a manner that "echoes" a famous self-murder, because proof-of-concept and defense-of-concept are such a drag. If I don't have the willpower to breathe another second, how do you expect me to supply the footnotes, bibliography, et cetera, required to demonstrate a person can or should die in such a way? And won't it make you happy to feel so smart about the condition of my death…come on, let's not lie to each other now.

Bothered in Bowie, Maryland 8/1/10
John Edward Lawson

Introduction: The Suicide's Soliloquy
by Abraham Lincoln

(published on August 25, 1838, *The Sangamo Journal*)

Here, where the lonely hooting owl
Sends forth his midnight moans,
Fierce wolves shall o'er my carcase growl,
Or buzzards pick my bones.

No fellow-man shall learn my fate,
Or where my ashes lie;
Unless by beasts drawn round their bait,
Or by the ravens' cry.

Yes! I've resolved the deed to do,
And this the place to do it:
This heart I'll rush a dagger through,
Though I in hell should rue it!

Hell! What is hell to one like me
Who pleasures never knew;
By friends consigned to misery,
By hope deserted too?

To ease me of this power to think,
That through my bosom raves,
I'll headlong leap from hell's high brink,
And wallow in its waves.

Though devils yell, and burning chains
May waken long regret;
Their frightful screams, and piercing pains,
Will help me to forget.

Yes! I'm prepared, through endless night,
To take that fiery berth!
Think not with tales of hell to fright
Me, who am damn'd on earth!

Sweet steel! come forth from your sheath,
And glist'ning, speak your powers;
Rip up the organs of my breath,
And draw my blood in showers!

I strike! It quivers in that heart
Which drives me to this end;
I draw and kiss the bloody dart,
My last—my only friend!

Judges 16:29 Then Samson reached toward the two central pillars on which the temple stood. Bracing himself against them, his right hand on the one and his left hand on the other,

30 Samson said, "Let me die with the Philistines!" Then he pushed with all his might, and down came the temple on the rulers and all the people in it. Thus he killed many more when he died than while he lived.

You Will Not Meet Me

When we bump into each other
on the street, when we are
introduced by an acquaintance,
when we are pressed together
by the tides of a party: you will
not meet me. Not halfway, nor
a third. Your vision is blurred
by the retroviral
suspicion that I could be
a degenerate descendant of Yahwe's
anger and remorse. My approach
is cloaked in a rotten egg
smell that begs the question
Did somebody pull God's finger?

You will not greet me.
Despite the countless lumens
exuding from my pores a darkness
slips through, eclipsing your
smile. You will be assured
I am merely dirty from my travels,
my long fall before deplaning,
my meat slow-smoked and full
of carcinogens, soot circling
in my eyes.

You will not embrace me.
Instead your vigorous hand-
shakes sweat and suffocate
within the confines of your jockstrap.
The back-pat of camaraderie
is tucked away in the pocket
of your other jacket, the one that fell

victim to a Korean dry cleaning conspiracy.
The brittle peck on the cheek
is stuffed in your bra,
its sincerity enough only to fill
one side, the mastectomy
of etiquette.

You will not meet me
.000000000000001 to the 10 billionth power %
of the way. What necessitates this
calculus of avoidance? What cultural
steroids were administered to make
you + me practically non-Euclidian
in scope? This withering
divisibility, this non-reciprocal
subtraction, this utterly predictable
stiletto massage administered
with intimate familiarity.

You will remember
some man, some pretender, some
time you wish had not been
wasted, soiled by misrepresentation.
But you will remember.

Friends of Virginia W.

My name is John and I'm a failure
addict. If you put it
in front of me I will
pop it, smoke it, eat it, drink
it with no questions or
hesitation. If it moves
I will stick myself into
it, without reservation or
invitation. If my future
or my family depend on it I will
abstain; discretion is the worst
part of failure.

Too many of you also know what
it means to be afflicted
with the wrong people at too
early an age: the ones who
drag you into their own
vices by demonstration, by
coercion…the ones who
cultivate the splintered
bonsai of your heart, pruning
away inhibition, composting
reason. The ones who plant
their seed of shame in your
eyes, staining everything
with the tint of
your own pain.

I am the incomplete abortion
of too many schemers, an
orgy of thieves. Today is
my first day but it

feels like it will
be my last.

Today always will
and always has.

So I'm praying for the strength
that should have been lent
by elders in my youth, when
instead they invested their
weakness in me. I pray for
the strength to repay both
the principal and the interest,
and the wisdom not to…but:

My name is John.
And
I'm a failure addict.

Acts 16:27 The jailer woke up, and when he saw the prison doors open, he drew his sword and was about to kill himself because he thought the prisoners had escaped.

Memory = Perception, Perception < Choice

The sun in your eyes, the world's breath
in your hair, and fields of smiles sown
along the road from our car to the seventh
state fair at the horizon's vanishing point, grown
to be my mode, median, and mean. My everything.

In the glow of the dashboard the cream
of your expression hangs in darkness, framed
by the absence of a destination's lack of meaning.
With me as your husband every arrival is the same,
and the fact of you at my side justifies my ears, eyes.

The reality of your flesh and bone, your weight
a comfort that my luck is real. Your scent
something like melon and dust and a boundless landscape
of veils and Sunday hats and the burnt incense of Lent.
The velvet spike of your gaze strips calendars of days.

This envelope of comfort we travel within
was never sealed with your saliva, or mine,
and breathless hope wheezes its final admonition:
you would never reveal—or help to suicide—
the part of me that knows you were not the one I chose.

First/Last Fumble

You believe that because you have a weapon you are dangerous.
It is without weapons that you are safe-less.

Breathing, eating, buying, consumering as a defense.
Speaking your nonsense—or, worse still, sense.

You believe that I should be afraid of you.
For all the reasons ticked off on your flesh-sticks, I could add a few.

They have, combined, mind you, a miscegenation of illness-symmetry.
That is, the facts of your deadliness = the facts of my own lethality.

Neither of us owns a monopoly on rage, vengeance.
Let us barter, then, and enter a free trade agreement.

Come now, it is time to drink wine and make love…
before I agree to kill you, and you agree to kill John Edward Lawson.

I never thought I would make it past 30
Every day I live is overtime
All actions I take are sudden-death
Penalties lurk within each new breath

Every day I live is overtime
As I near 40 years of doing this
Penalties lurk within each new breath
That 20-something drags behind me, purpling

As I near 40 years of doing this
They don't call it killing yourself, it's "reinvention"
That 20-something drags behind me, purpling
A youngster refuses digestion in my belly

They don't call it killing yourself, it's "reinvention"
All actions I take are sudden-death
A youngster refuses digestion in my belly
I never did make it past 30

My Boy

You may be wondering, son, why
this had to happen…did you really need
to read this? And where
have I been? Lost

in the wilderness of my own screams,
unreasoning anger petrified
by love's Medusa-stare.
My will crumbles long before those snaking branches.

Son, where have I been? Stretched
on the barbed memory of throwing
you down in frustration; your
inability to sleep woke your mother

to wrath, and running low
on manhood I passed that fury on
down the line. Where have I
been, little one? Staring

at the best part of me, escaped
and set loose in a world
of soot and anguish, and my helping
hand withheld by spite. Where

have I been? Lost in means of avoidance
when you most needed my guidance.
When I was young I did not
defend my virtue with enough vigor,

losing patience first. I let you down
while you insisted on giving me more
chances. Where have I been?

Digging my grave and jumping in

only to shatter both my legs
because I fouled up the depth of it.
But perhaps this isn't a screw-up; where
have I been? Passing the shovel to you.

Matthew 4:5 Then the devil took him to the holy city and had him stand on the highest point of the temple.

Matthew 4:6 "If you are the Son of God," he said, "throw yourself down. For it is written: "'He will command His angels concerning you, and they will lift you up in their hands, so that you will not strike your foot against a stone.'"

Concrete Operational Thinking

To be boring is a kind
of raucous self-murder
slowly stalking one childhood
dream after another, binding
teenage aspirations to the
steel table in Freud's basement

Tracing a ruby Y along the svelte
torso of adulthood's jubilant
release, from the authority
of parents and instructors
with the scalpel of truth:

That we cannot relinquish our
grasp on concrete limitations
no matter how cold or deep
the flow of life gets

Job 15:11 Are God's consolations not enough for you,
    words spoken gently to you?

Right to Bear Self-Murder

NRA does not stand
for Niggers Run Away
although race may
also dance on that
two-edged blade
No, see, today

we discuss the epidemiology
of a clandestine death
cult society
barreling down on you and me
spannng across the country

NRA will get at us
with its right-to-death apparatus
and while the messenger may be spastic
the message is not erratic
so let's cleave through the media static:

Not Right Alive
is assisted suicide
Insisting on the right
to defend myself
from me and I
So when it comes to
the right to die
movement there's no
need to legalize
Euthanasia advocacy
is all about
demand and supply

NOT—RIGHT—ALIVE

If you're alive you
ain't right
and NRA wants to
help with that
Well, homey
don't play scat
Don't play
the rat-tat-tat-tat
Don't make fiction
into fact
because crap
is just that
just us
without justice
just us
without a lobbyist
to lob this: TRUTH

Because shit does
roll downhill
especially on
Capitol Hill
or should I say
Capitalizing on the Ill
because the populace
cannot afford a lobbyist
to stand up and say
"Don't help us!
"Don't push
the self-inflicted
gunshot death rate
past 60% of all
suicides this year
even if it means profits
drop this quarter!"
Because money talks

and shit rolls downhill
—when it comes to gravity
Smith & Wesson
could skeet Newton
every time.
In alphebetic code
NRA takes the issue global
making us part of the NWO:
Neurotic Without Objectivity
Or to put it simply
We're all FINE:
Fucked-up, Insecure,
Neurotic, and Emotional
And that has to be the goal
That has to be the cost
A thing we
gave up on
Something
long lost
A Rosetta stoned
alphabet of
U and I
replacing
N and
R and
A

Some Windows Cannot Be Closed

The girl watches from across the street
as you sell stolen goods, and you want
to impress her, so when your friends
want to creep up in some new crib you go

as you sell stolen goods, and you want
it over quickly so she can see you
Want to creep up in some new crib, you go
through a broken window without cutting yourself

It's over quickly: she can see you
with eyes that will never close again
escape through a broken window without cutting yourself
and your friends wonder what's up

With eyes that will never close again
you see the corpse with shards in her wrists,
and your friends wonder what's up…
the girl watches from across the street

Life, LLC Promotion Lvl 4

This is the job
at four years of age:
polish father's shoes
matching the colors
of Kiwi Wax and leather,
making note of subtle
differences—not difficulties—
in the brush types.
Don't forget the edge
of father's sole.
Sort the family's dirty
clothes, carry them
to the laundry machine
and don't jam
the quarter slot.
Don't use too much
detergent, and try
not to drink any.
Understand how to read
the clock so you know when
to dry the clothes.
Comprehend when and how
to sweep with a broom
or vacuum; ensure the
pattern left behind
is consistent, despite
the retrieved-from-trash-
dumpster nature of said
carpet. Know which variety
of tile requires Comet
for cleaning, and which
necessitates Mop 'n Glow
…don't forget one

is applied on hands and knees
using a sponge, the other
with a mop. Get it through
your skull when to accept
that foreign tongue pressed
into your mouth,
and when to pretend it doesn't
happen. Assist by foraging
for "found food objects."
Kill roaches no matter
what the circumstance.
Don't you want the job?
Every time your parents
tag off to enter the arena
of "tonight I die" jump
to and save them, look
alive. You don't get paid
for nothing. Forgo
games and TV for hours
of travel to the doctors
and surgeons and hours more
waiting to hear
if the procedure was successful.
Pretend the invisible nature
of all extended family
does not bother you
or your parents.
Keep quiet about being
forced to look at those
dirty magazines. Oh no-no,
you question the benefits?
What's this about overtime?
Ingrate! You forgot
to wash the windows and mirrors
starting at the top, working
your way to the bottom.

Know your way around
a can of Pledge? Good.
Now polish that wood.
Take out the trash,
by which I mean make
three trips up and down
the elevator hauling
bags as big as yourself.
Father's corn has needs
involving little hands
and a tiny cheese grater
during his baths. Carry
groceries and other goods
a mile or two home
with your mother every week
due to your family's inability
to own a car until you are
16—we'll discuss that
at a later date.
This is the job.
Congratulations, my boy,
your work ethic makes us
proud. Perhaps next year
you can handle additional
responsibilities. And the year
after that, and the year after
that, and the year after that.
Don't ever dare dream
of making management, though…
you'll break long
before that.
Heh-heh. Back
to your ghetto activities
now, we only have so much time
before we drive you
into the ground.

The planned obsolescence
of childhood, we call it.
Oh, I almost forgot:
figure out how to clean sinks
and tubs, but not toilets.
That would be too much
to ask of a child. That,
and washing dishes.
We're counting on you!
Go make us proud.

Job 6:8 "Oh, that I might have my request,
    that God would grant what I hope for,

9 that God would be willing to crush me,
    to let loose his hand and cut me off!

Maximum Entropy Model

The enemy's face is known to me
for it needs not don a mask
Ubiquitous and disquieting, it stares
daily, stalking hourly, bearing down
every minute, stealing the seconds
from my lungs with each tick of its hands

Job 3:11 "Why did I not perish at birth,
    and die as I came from the womb?

Seventh (Healing) Circle

Spring's breath aches through the nettles far removed
from prying eyes and mouths that can meddle
Those who went before remain unsettled
and scattered, their chalky frames ground to dust
If there is peace it is found in all rest…
be the bed consecrated or unblessed

Job 20 "Why is light given to those in misery,
    and life to the bitter of soul,

21 to those who long for death that does not come,
    who search for it more than for hidden treasure,

22 who are filled with gladness
    and rejoice when they reach the grave?

Anti-Christening

Sol staggers treacherously high
to glare down on the shadowy
details of *her* last day, but
all she sees is vapor burning away,
the fog lifting, shredded by
heavenly fishhooks. The tension evaporates
as her skin warms, draped with hope
and terminal knowledge: she will
never endure this again.

She enters the convenience mart with a forgotten
smile. Once she purchased headaches
and digestive upset in the form of
hot drinks and greasy, sweet food there every day,
though it has been a while. Too long. The gaudy
decor and stock have not produced
such a shock for quite some time,
have not brewed this vibrant
reverberation in her mind. Perhaps a stymie
has been removed from her eye?

The post office's tentacles uncoil
in welcome, and birdsong penetrates
her ear. This one last time the clerks
are infested with…could that be
cheer? The pills, razor, and gun
hunger for her at home; Florence works
the postage meter while recalling her children,
grandchildren, plants, cats, and troublesome dears.
For once the brutality of mundane conversation
is tolerable. Tomorrow she will not be
here, she will not hear.

Couples in the store, the park,
the street…they dissolve into the scenery.
They would have melted the lining
of her stomach previously. Infants marauding
through aisles in strollers, cawing
in the parking lot, she knows they see
a zombie, a teaser of the violent
end, a fact that fills her mouth with a sweet
tune to sing.

On returning library books a final time
the bounce in her step provides
such a contrast to the dour librarians
and patrons that she wants to do it
once more. She plucks a volume or nine from
the shelves and braves the wait
in line. She feels herself swaying in time
with the kelp in the brine, the birds of prey
spiraling through the sky, in step
with the natural flow of things. Her
face shines and everybody offers
a pleasant greeting.

At home the implements of her exit
go unused. It comes to mind there are
other loose ends she neglected. Her final
hour is reset, shifted back a day.
After suffering thousands of them
what's one more? The sun greets her
again, but strangely the ten tons of
familiar agony do not beset her. Instead
it feels as though she has won a far-fetched
bet. It dawns on her the "good" known
previously was not as good as it gets.

Without realization she becomes

a last-day addict. The weapons remain
home, stood up for date after date, while she
faces each sunrise alone but high
on the knowledge it will be her last.
And her last has grown into a week, a month,
year, end zone and end zone
celebrated in even as she just passes through.
You can be a gambler even though your dice remain unthrown.

Proof

Sometimes
I just need
to forget
I do exist
in order
to ensure
I continue
to exist

1 Chronicles 10:4 Saul said to his armor-bearer, "Draw your sword and run me through, or these uncircumcised fellows will come and abuse me."
    But his armor-bearer was terrified and would not do it; so Saul took his own sword and fell on it.

5 When the armor-bearer saw that Saul was dead, he too fell on his sword and died.

Untitled

You know what? There
was some effort, or
at least the intention
of some exertion, at
some point. But everything
is rendered ridiculous
within seconds of focus.
Wouldn't it be

wonderful if this was
due to some extraordinary
intellect, a ponderous jewel
weighing down my crown
with such insistence that
its gravity snaps my neck.
Accomplishments mutate
into mundanity, the
lycanthropy of life-hate:

yes, I am a life-ist.
This establishmentarian
reserves the right to refuse
servitude to life in any
shade or shape. Animation
is the life-man's burden,
and while the life-ist
movement is not politically
correct it is growing,

with new recruits every day, the
efforts of each underscoring
how meaningless effort
really is.

It's Rude to Point

Your friends are angry
because you mention the attack
helicopter hovering over the other
street, and the children accompanying
those adults under fire. They tell
you the bullets and explosives are
only landing on people who should have
known better than to stand on that block.
None of you have ever walked that stretch
of road, but if it were the one you
lived on you certainly would not go outside.
Your friends argue they would not point
up at the helicopter shouting to fellow
insurgents, nor try to take images
of the occurrence. Your friends raise
fingers directing your attention to the justice
being served, and they assure you the right
side is winning this thing. Their word
choices are civil, but it's a sure bet
the next time your friends see you on
the street they'll pretend not to. You remember
when the city spent almost $12 million
on the attack helicopter, and millions more on
training the crew, and how the tree-huggers
were so pissy about the over-a-half-mil-per-mission
cost, and the bitching about how many
missions were run per day, and how they talked
nonsense about that money coming out of your
children's mouths when it's the undesirables
who are trying to take money out of
your children's mouths. You don't mention
these thoughts to your friends, because
it would be rude to interrupt their continued

censure of your inappropriate questions. Yes,
you understand that—as your friends have
pointed out several times—there's no way
to know what intel led the helicopter to open
fire on the pedestrians, just as well as you
know it would be improper to point out
the helicopter turning, approaching behind
your friends now, sights being trained on th—

1 Kings 16:18 When Zimri saw that the city was taken, he went into the citadel of the royal palace and set the palace on fire around him. So he died…

Mazel Tov Cocktail

The rope of pus-infused mucous
pulled from his wound by the nurse is not
enough for him to erect a makeshift
gallows to finish the job. Perhaps
he should be as thankful as they
tell him he should be. If he dares to
voice his suffering they will not hesitate
to chastise him with asides about
the pediatric oncology ward, the burn
unit. Failed suicides do not rank.

Strangers drift in and out, as does
consciousness…well-wishers, support
group recruiters, those proselytizing
on behalf of pantheons or monotheisms.
Each is both a surprise and expected,
an encouragement and a disappointment.
Well after visiting hours are over
a man slips in. The patient sharing
the room has been hauled off, and the staff
are busy tending bleed-outs down the way.

"Congrats are in order," the stranger
says, proffering a wine bottle. "You
managed to survive despite the fact
that people who want life get it cut
short every day." The man ignites
what looks to be a tampon stuffed
into the bottle top, counts, and smashes
it on the hospital cot, incinerating
the failed suicide. He exits without
obstruction, his vigilanteism lending
to self-murder a new dimension of terror.

History 101
Prof. LaValley
Wilson State University, Lakeside Campus

A Brief History of Mummies
by Ronald Darin Densman

Mummies existed in the area now known as Egypt until several thousand years ago. They became extinct because they were arrogant and did not teach God's law in school. As established by Focault, "...[mummies] deserved to die." (*Gestalt and the No-Fault Engagement of Civil Disobedience*, Aylett & Beard, 1999)

Current evidence points to a rise and decline in the Mummy Empire dating from 8,967 years before the birth of our Lord and Savior Jesus Christ to 1,009 years before the birth of our Lord and Savior Jesus Christ. (Wikipedia, all et al, 2010) The boundaries of the Mummy Empire at its height ranged from Sudan in the south to Tunisia in the west, Syria in the north to Sumeria in the east. On the eastern front they suffered many battles against the armies of Gozer the Gozarian. (*An Illuminating Treatise on the Origins of the Supernatural and the Subnatural*, Venkman et al, 1984) Soon afterwards the Mummy empire shrank to the area immediately surrounding the Nile and its tributaries.

An underlying cause of this decline is the fact they worshipped a god whose johnson fell off and floated down a river. People who worship a johnsonless god are assholes. Even experts agree, as deposited in Shipp's "Theorem of Mummies Are Assholes." (*Supernatural Assholery of Historic Proportions*, Shipp et al, 2008)

Based on the above observations I have decided to become a mummy. (*A Brief History of Mummies*, Densman et al, 2010) With my recently acquired contemporary and even modern knowledge of the subject I have an advantage over the mummies who existed in ignorance many histories ago. On top of that, the God I worship has maintained his johnson—which is why it is so scary when televangelists warn us "God has taken away his protection." (*700 Club*, Oral Roberts et al, 2001) That is, in the context of a spiritual rubber.

I went on eBay figuring I could secure a mummy's-worth of bandages in a bulk lot, but shipping is cost-prohibitive and the recent cotton scourge (*Farmer's Almanac*, Farmer et al, 2010) has driven up production costs. Instead I will make use of thousands of Band-Aids purchased at my local wholesale superstore.

Also, it is worth noting that while I could not find a sarcophagus to buy or steal, and both the students and instructors in the art department told me to "go away" (snobby bitches et al, yesterday) a viable solution has been found by taking a 150-gallon fishtank and spraypainting it gold. A papíer maché of my face is glued on top. I even added that weird penis-looking goatee on my chin. Why do the sarcophagi always have those penis-beards, but the mummies never do? Because they could not even maintain a facial johnson, that is why.

Eternity will be mine. Mummies were negroes, or half-breeds at best, while I am a White Man of legally Caucasian mind and body, a fact that empowers me to do whatever I want. Sorry Professor, but after my resurrection Debbie the T.A. is mine.

My body is waiting in the student apartments at XX XXXXXX XX XXX X. I took the hemlock, wolfsbane, and opium mixture Cleopatra used to kill herself while preserving her body. (ZDF, Schaefer, 2009) There you will find mason jars lined up on the kitchen counter; do not place them in the dishwasher. These are to be used in place of canopic jars. Instructions for the embalming and organ removal process are attached (see Appendix 1) as well as the drying process and wrapping process (see Appendix 2). Good luck, and don't mess up or I'll destroy your family with sick Mummy spells.

In conclusion, since I am a Christian my soul will still be a part of God's Kingdom after death, but my body will stay here and FSU (Fuck Shit Up). Using the Law of God Almighty I will establish a proper Mummy dynasty in short order without any question, making the defense of my thesis a cakewalk. I know that you'll give me at least a C+ for this term paper, so I'm not worried about grades, but make sure to use extra Band-Aids on the johnson region, or else Debbie the T.A. will be useless to me.

kaishakunin

How shall I stab you, brother?
Perhaps Mishima's blade will
do. Would you like it in the head,
or is insertion from the rear
preferable? There, there;
you make a formfitting sheath.
Try not to squirm when my tip
stirs back and forth sounding
the mortal depths of your vessel,
birthing a scalding coffee cup
swirl of white and brown and white
nondairy creamer sweetened
by anguish. Now you! Employ your
bayonet to take a whack or three
at my throat. Can you
sever my mind from my heart, sweet
one? Is your masculinity up
to the task, or does it call
for a militia of brothers? That
may be best, the desirable strength
of numbers. Gather them all up
for a bukakke of arterial spray,
harvest them to reap us. Care
to sacrifice the boys before we go?
Hellfire…they have all been kamikazeed
by cabinet members, those virgin
killers we elected to firebomb
our fears across to the far side
of oblivion. They sold Persephone
the winning PowerBall ticket,
allowing her to buy Cousin Sam, Jr.
into her stead—how I had longed
to explore his incision. Probably

for the best, that. Dying is
the province of men, love is
earmarked for adults, and this pact
augments our standing as both,
even while nullifying it.

Job 16:11 God has turned me over to evil men
    and thrown me into the clutches of the wicked.

12 All was well with me, but he shattered me;
    he seized me by the neck and crushed me.
    He has made me his target;

13 his archers surround me.
    Without pity, he pierces my kidneys
    and spills my gall on the ground.

14 Again and again he bursts upon me;
    he rushes at me like a warrior.

bilanz Selbstmord

Expectant the pain should recede,
a neural low tide revealing
artifacts of malignancy,
she is surprised—but not
disappointed—when it refuses.

They knew this time would
come. Prepared for it with all
the vigilance and future-tense
love of bringing a child into
the world. But the door swings

both ways. Her physician confirms
the time is near. Does she resent
him for denying her a rash,
violent end? For talking her
down from the heights of fear?

The two hundred ten days that have
cycled though the span between then
and now were some of the most
joy-drenched of her life. Her
accounts settled she embraces

him with the last of her vigor,
thankful that she did not have to
call in his promise to end it if
she could not endure, and that he
made the offer to begin with.

"We are only gifted
with this experience once,"
she whispers to him.

"You have allowed me to know it,
and to die an adult because of it."

He nods, smiling into
her pain-numbed eyes.
She goes.

Job 15 20 All his days the wicked man suffers torment,
    the ruthless through all the years stored up for him.

21 Terrifying sounds fill his ears;
    when all seems well, marauders attack him.

22 He despairs of escaping the darkness;
    he is marked for the sword.

23 He wanders about—food for vultures;
    he knows the day of darkness is at hand.

24 Distress and anguish fill him with terror;
    they overwhelm him, like a king poised to attack…

Struggle Session

History does not favor the meek.
Misfortune, ruin, and death do.
I choose to be bold.

I fear not premature demise,
but immature demise.

Matthew 27:5 So Judas threw the money into the temple and left. Then he went away and hanged himself.

Acts 1:18 With the reward he got for his wickedness, Judas bought a field; there he fell headlong, his body burst open and all his intestines spilled out.

On the Re-Gifting of Souls

What does it take to be
damned in this world? When sin
coils around every wrist and
every ankle begetting a nation
of slaves, when blasphemy drips
from every pair of lips?
The journey to end pain instead
of prolonging its intensity
is enough to earn placement
in Hell. How dare we deny
such a gift?

Infidel(ity)

Death's swaggar is not
born of ill-crafted pride
or drunkeness induced by fermented
sweat and gall—while Death may
imbibe now and again, gluttony
is not involved. No, Death's
stride is symptomatic of
testicular elephantitis. The
condition was brought on by
Death's legendary promiscuity.
That homewrecker, always
desiring what is unavailable.
But still Death beckons, "Come
to me, darling." Scratching
at the door. "We can be
together." Scratching at the window.
"It would be so easy to leave them
all behind." Scratching at your
skin. Once Death has you it moves
on; Death desires sexual
congress with your polyps, fibroids,
prolapsed uterus drained
of life, drools over your
broken hip sashay. But the grass
is always yellower in the yard
of another. In the forrest of
Death's exes the wood you gave it
was particle board at best.

Another Day, Another Dollar

The weight of the day
seeks a way in, rattles
windows and doors and bones,
insistent in its hunger

A lead pillar of shame
rests on my chest, brittle
resolve and knowledge goes
for cover, dissipating thunder

The pressure mounts
me in this bed, seeks a
way inside, assisted by
binding blankets and sheets

There is no air for sound
and there exists no escape,
no truth to combat daylight,
only the legacy of my screams

The strain presses its blade
to my throat, promising
if I behave it won't kill me,
it won't leave any scars

The butcher's scale ticks away
seconds in silent witness, stiff
as every element in this crime scene;
the sun's beams are prison bars

I put my trust in you
Tomorrow, and you came as promised
You planted hope in me

Tomorrow, and I arrived compromised

I put my trust in you
Tomorrow, there's blood on the mattress
You planted hope in me
Tomorrow, the blood will outlast us

1 Kings 19:4 While he himself went a day's journey into the desert. He came to a broom tree, sat down under it and prayed that he might die. "I have had enough, LORD," he said. "Take my life; I am no better than my ancestors."

Perverted Uncle on Park Bench

A Parasitic Jaeger approaches
with dark cap and pale underwings
twitching, taking another bite

I toss bread crumbs on the pavement
It does not judge me, nor do
the Iceland Gulls, the Orchard Orioles
Unlike suspicious neighbors

Even my family accused me of baking
in poison to amuse myself…this time
when I tear off a piece it's my turn
to chew

Revelation 9:6 During those days men will seek death, but will not find it; they will long to die, but death will elude them.

Chick Magnet

The car is red
Freud would turn away
Is Jack okay with that?
There's no need to ask, just take a look
All attention is drawn to him as he cruises
Clearly looking for flesh and ready to get raw

A sexy stranger presses herself against the car
and Jack smiles, but before he can let her in
another sexy stranger arrives, and another
Not only can Jack not accommodate them all
but soon the weight taxes his suspension
He attempts to speed away and only succeeds
in creating extra helpings of hairy road sauce
With tendons, belts, and scrunchies wrapped
around the wheels his driveshaft ruptures
Gouts of smoke and blood erupt from his tailpipe
—he'll need more than a lube job to fix that
And still the women appear, throwing themselves
at Jack, coating him with their bodily fluids
as his sex machine hobbles away, a success

Clearly, look at the flesh, bloody and raw
All attention is drawn to him as he cruises
There's no need to ask, just take a look
Is Jack okay with that?
Freud would turn away
The car is red

I promise not to
come back as a
vampire or other supernatural
reminder of your failure

and mine, so please
don't bury me at
the crossroads to look
up skirts and tailpipes

And Dreams Take Flight

                                  It is her first time

Struggling to stand
against the constant
wind, sealing her lips
to keep her breath safe

                                  It is her first time

The World's mouth
gaping below her,
waiting for unsure footing
to feed its grumbling schadenfreude

                                  He has done it before

The collection of exterior
scars rivals his internal
assortment, but the softness
in his eyes puts her at ease

                                  He has done it before

Not even in the present anymore
his heart has already crossed
over, bitter failures
at last breeding success

                                  It is their last time

Meeting atop a suspension
bridge seems almost
providence, and they share
a smile knowing "what could be"

                                  It is their last time

Opting instead
for one long
step together
into a certain cessation of hostility

Seppuku

staring into coffins
friends comfortable at long last
close my eyes

flakey crust sizzles
half-baked meat's pungent aroma
cranial exit wound

Jumping off a cliff
Cannonball without a war
The blood is a pool

Slice up, not sideways
One final lesson…for whom?
Morticians cut deep

Sudden wind blast lives
just a moment in your nerves
before the impact

Dosage may vary
depending on the level
of pain you desire

Skin, fat, muscle, blood;
like layers of an onion
they leave you crying

Untitled

Suicide, Suicide
I must ask you why
You are the perfect rhyme
And the imperfect crime

There once was a goth from Nantucket
Who cut out her voice box and plucked it
    The melancholy sound
    drew a frivolous crowd
It was a bitter pill, but she sucked it

I can't bring myself to do it
Despite the tears I can see through it
In the verses of life vs. strife
As a poet I blew it

Numbers 11:15 If this is how you are going to treat me, put me to death right now—if I have found favor in your eyes—and do not let me face my own ruin.

Sin-Cain(s)

Suicide
Faded energy
Draining, slowing, exploding
Its own short life
Exhausted

Steel bridge
Cold gray bearer
Of lovers and mourners
Leaping…an unfilled void remains
Crossed

Skyscraper
Soot-stained
Looming, unyielding, plummeting
Radio tower impales clouds
Monstrosity

Railroad
Unstoppable, impartial
grinding, churning, spewing
Left him no choice
Framed

Garden
Lush adornment
We prune, aerate, dig, scrape
Where the heart is
Buried

A Death Less Ordinary

1.
At what moment is
tea perfectly brewed? If
it has steeped too

long, is not even
bitterness a gift? Perhaps
moreso than subtle

sweetness…
do not gulp too
greedily.

2.
After standing proud
as a flag all these years, what
will become of us
when the wind is stilled? No
one can judge our slack wrinkles.

3.
The irrigation
trenches, a source of illness
when not maintained, are
replaced by new sustenance.
Fields continue regardless.

4.
Does bacteria
have remorse? Which smile is
smaller: virus, lion?
Both devour others, but only
one consumes everything.

5.
Reefs are visible
at low tide only. I gaze
upon the high tide.
It is enough just to know
what lies beyond the surface.

6.
The hawk that rockets
from view does not cease to be;
beyond the smoky
horizon it frolics, swoops
down on things we cannot know.

7.
The reading was wonderful, Joan.
Thank you.
*Gerald would have loved
to hear his final words
conveyed with such passion and understanding.*
I think so too. It was lovely.
*And printing them
in the memorial book! We're all
going to be poring over those
verses for some time
to come.*
So will I. They meant so much to him.
Japanese, was it? The style I mean.
**Yes. I can't remember
the official name for it now. Maybe
later. The basic style is called
Tanka.**
Like the trucks.
[awkward chuckle]
*Anyways. I'll let you get
on, I know you've got plenty*

of people to greet. And let me
know, dear, if I can ever help
you in any way. You hear?
Thank you, Hattie.
Pardon me, ma'am. I realize
this may not be the right time
but I represent a publishing
house and we heard about
this beautiful poetry
all the way up in New
York. We hope to make
your husband's contributions
to the literary world permanent…

8.
Narita-san sat across
from Gerald, curious that
a foreigner would understand
so much of Japan's proud

literary tradition. Jisei
no ku: the Japanese death
poem. "Once upon a time,"

Narita-san mused, "it was
common to seek the advice

of masters on composing
one's own death poem."
He poured fresh matcha

for himself…and his guest.
Gerald thanked him, then

nodded. *I was diagnosed*
with pancreatic cancer.

I have one to three months

if I'm lucky. Narita-san
sighed. "It is touching

you would travel across
the world in order to
secure this kind of legacy.

What may I do to help?"
Exactly what Higa-san, Hamada-

*san, Miyake-san, Inoue-san,
and Goto-san did.* "Wait—you
have already consulted with

the other grand masters? Why
would you need to speak with

me? And how could that be true,
considering their deaths?"
Narita-san, I mean no disrespect,

*but I have no experience either
writing or killing myself. A*

*surrogate is what I need,
for credit in one area and
experimentation in the other.*

Narita-san finally understood
why so many greats "committed

suicide" at the height of their
powers, and why they left no
jisei no ku of their own.

Gerald placed a pen on the table
with paper and blade. He

smiled…sickly, dangerously.

My Death, or: Get Some!!

My death is a star-studded affair
      with thalidomide love children to spare
My death will steal your breath
      and give it to the poor
My death is every masculinist beating his breast
      even while cowering behind locked doors
My death is the gender reassignment your surgeon
      turned in late because his dog ate it
My death is enough to blind Charon
      like the time Cerberus' mother mated
My death is 36,000,000 fruit bats seppukuing
      the apple of your eye with rabies-dripping incisors
My death is every politician renewing
      their lease on life without ever becoming buyers
My death sips iron-studded disembowelments
      and bleeds laughter between wind-blown teeth
My death is in the market for rent-controlled apartments
      overlooking valleys of milkless teats
My death is bigger than your death, *mon frère*
      but is preoccupied with its own health scare
My death is.

How To Be a Good Guy

Expend your family's youth bouncing
from nation to nation, bartering the tender
years of your sons and wife for subversion.
Try to buy leaders and organizations,
then attempt to bully them. When all
else fails cultivate an insurgency by locating
the intellectually outrageous, the emotionally
unrighteous. Give them anger and weapons
and a working knowledge of how to stop
up sewage and every other societal infrastructure,
shake them up in a bag and unleash
them; pack up and move. In the next
culture you introduce drugs and nab anyone
you can off the streets. Keep them caged
for "interrogation classes" with a handful
of the insurgency's best and brightest.
Sustain the "lives" of your teaching tools
for terse weeks, rigid months, wilting years
if you can. Dump the bodies where they will be
found and arrange for charity groups to cite
the corpses as evidence of human rights
abuses. Now the shakedown target is known
as a "regime" and Congress offers tacit
support to your death squads. Job well
done. Medal award ceremony in private.
Move the family stateside and go abroad
occasionally for short jaunts like Tiananmen
Square. A couple years later your son is dating
an Asian girl in college and dies in a way
that forces not only a cover story for his demise
but your full-time return to the international
arena. You join in the late teen years and never
really retire. Not until you are diagnosed. With

what little time you have left you dump
every crime against humanity you committed
in the lap of a priest, then pull the trigger
in the privacy of your car.

Job 3:1 After this, Job opened his mouth and cursed the day of his birth.

2 He said:

3 "May the day of my birth perish,
    and the night it was said, 'A boy is born!'

4 That day—may it turn to darkness;
    may God above not care about it;
    may no light shine upon it.

5 May darkness and deep shadow claim it once more;
    may a cloud settle over it;
    may blackness overwhelm its light.

Survival Ritual

1
Think of your loved one's voice
and the smell of their hair
and the sensation of them against your skin
Think of your loved one's face
and the way they looked at you
and the shape of their mouth in anger, in joy
Close your eyes, breathe in, breathe out
This is life, and you survive
You survive

2
See your loved one in dreams
interacting in the familiar ways,
or doing things you never did together,
but knowing they are with you all the same
Wake to darkness or light
and the realization that it was not real
Release the choked feeling, the tears
This is life, and you survive
You survive

3
The actions of others swirl too fast
during consciousness, then slow to a freeze-frame
and none of it seems within your control, your ability to comprehend
And none of it seems related to your loved one
except there's one less person to lean on,
one less door to pass through
Close your eyes, breathe in, breathe out, wipe the sweat away
This is life, and you survive
You survive

4
The restaurant you went to with your loved one
darkens the street's landscape
so you grow accustomed to taking alternate routes
And certain pages in your recipe book—
as well as particular spots in the grocery store—
induce blank spots of time when you catch yourself standing, confused
Release the choked feeling, take in that nourishment once again
This is life, and you survive
You survive

5
Keep something that belonged to your loved one
somewhere in your line of sight
at work or at home
If anybody should ask about the item
speak freely, without hesitation
and without the spin of a publicity campaign
Breathe easily, stay focused
This is life, and you survive
You survive

Burning Sylvia Plath's Bra

Because you died in 1963,
Sylvia, you were never in life
liberated; five years and the abyss'
yawning divide separated you from the famous
Miss America Pageant protests. What would
you have made of those female hundreds
tossing undergarments into the "Freedom Trash Can?"

Having traveled here to Heptonstall
Churchyard I am answered with silence
until popping the kerosene can open.
The shovel is dejected, its work done,
and the gallows birds are tucked away
to gorge on dreams of you. Not to begrudge
physical labor, but delving past the decorations
and outright vandalism of your groupies
was almost as annoying as the stab of
petrol fumes fumes violating nostrils.
Honey, I'm here to tell you your crew is
running thicker than some cervical mucous;
even Jim Morrison would be hard
pressed to compete with such adoration.

To make the grave robbing literal in more ways than one:
this firesong is a conversation among the ruins
for you and I, not unlike two sisters of Persephone
transforming street song into a soliloquy
of the solipsist…or is this just a monologue
at 3 a.m. rewording a letter to a purist?
Here in this November graveyard the song for
a summer's day dissipates into dialog between ghost
and priest. Among all the dead dears this Alicante

lullaby circles into itself: a wreath for a bride,
an epitaph for fire and flower.

My luminous, destructive embrace slithers
over your no-fly zone, through fabric and bone
and the dustbags, as you called them, convert
oxygen one last time, resuscitating the flame.
The pops and crackles give life
to the larynx you sacrificed, hissing
at the death of your brassiere, but the device
is unnessesary, a vestige of primitive fashion,
because as the proverb goes: "silence is a woman's
best garment." But sayings should never be taken
too literally, such as "she's got one in the oven."

If you were Hindu you would believe
the body is composed of five elements,
and that with your life extinguished the underwire
pyre burning in your bosom would complete you,
allowing your spirit to journey beyond this world.
As it stands you were Unitarian Christian,
and brassieres were not, in reality, set alight,
but it all sounds so much more appealing that way.
Journalists conducted reproduction experiments
on the pageant protesters by stitching them onto
the already-popularized draft card burning, creating
a Siamese left-wing of Frankensteinian proportions,
punching up the headlines. And stripped of those
defenses incinerating you does appear increasingly
a pre-cannibalistic act, save for the fact
that the hipbone and thighbone do connect;
everything must be weighed into condemnation.

Allow the defense to ask:
was suicide the only Freedom Trash Can
available to women of your time? Did you mean to

throw your life away, or was it a case of dumpster-
diving gone amiss? Was the intent to browse
the petrified bubble gum of adolescents who
never reached adulthood, the soiled maroon
sponges and towels disposed of by tear-
drenched parents? Perhaps you merely intended
to stick your head in the oven to see
if that was a burning bra you smelled.
Instead it would seem you found something
left smoldering since well beyond
the Mungo Lady's time.

And how would you
have fared in that '68 pageant?
Judging from your stark, duotone
poses Nicole Kidman could pass
for your less unfortunate sister,
or perhaps the kind of genetic
upgrade you might have hoped for
in a daughter—if you subscribed
to the arbitrary standards of glance
and glare: the entirety of a woman's value,
experience, and potential struggling
to fill the half second before
eyes move on to other targets,
or if you subscribed to *Mademoiselle*
where you interned as a not-so-ugly
Betty before madness slipped in,
attempting to end your life,
succeeding in killing your periodical
career.

And how would you
perform in the talent spectacle
of the pageant? Would it be a
demonstration of how you satisfied

Ted's oral needs with hours of slaving
away in the kitchen, scalded and singed
by the oven while infants howled
at you, your expansive intellect slowly
reclaimed by oceans of greasy linoleum
in that chamber of domestic blitz?
What would best complete your
impersonation of the Sears & Roebuck
kitchen concubine: the maniacal grin
of mother's two-fisted helper, or
twin jagged rows of pink, puckered skin
along your inner wrists?

And how would you
pose for the skinsuit competition?
Naturally, you supplied the answer with your final
act, assuming "the position" on hands and knees
with troublesome head obscured by an oven-glass
figure, and—*my compliments to the chef*—
drawing attention to one succulent rump roast—

DOWN BOY DOWN BOY DOWN BOY DOWN

…this freedom from patriarchal reconstriction
I seek to bestow upon you must be
carried out with solemnity and dignity
but Sylvy, before you question the purity
of my intentions, check yourself
after you wrecked yourself. Suicide
with your children in the room next door? Really?
Even grading on a morality bell-jar-curve that's
gotta be down near the ding-dong portion.
So before you swaddle me with that bare-
toothed, judgmental stare as-seen-on-
the-Internet, recall that I am after all
a man and you were a woman.

And therein lays the withdrawal string
in the Gordian knot of your posthumous public life:
the masculinists and feminists alike
—not to mention desperate authors seeking
to manipulate you as a literary device—
disregard anything beyond your sex organs,
ensure that you are interpreted as a woman only,
not as a person. Which is to say
a human with the core needs and
experiences common to all living things,
because truths do tend to be genderless.
Which dredges up the all-too-familiar refrain:

She
wanted
it.

Not objectification or consignment
to the cubbyholes of stereotype. But
suicide is a statement of intent and
accusation and a control mechanism,
a single-use lever on the memory
machine immortalizing you as an act,
because it is those who march slaughterhouse-
tranquil into the nursing home's embrace
who are remembered in human terms, not as the mere
backdrop for a mode of death.

Since your hasty exit, Sylvia,
by and by gender is itself becoming a mode
of death. While draft-dodging hippies, aged
by compromise, watch Muslim children
irradiated with depleted uranium shells the Third
Wave of Feminism is a puddle muddying over
a million homeless teens, a Sargasso Sea
littered with clam shelters bearing the depleted

Venus of hope, dreams irradiated by OCD and OD.
So maybe you did not miss anything by leaving
us when you did, other than an arithmetic
lesson of one in five women trying to kill
themselves by age 20, and even the dimmest
bulb can illuminate your anatomy lesson: the hipbone
is connected to the thighbone, the thighbone to
the hambone, the hambone is in the oven, and your
best garment = don't breathe for fear of making
a sound, don't breathe…you might blow out
the pilot light.

Liebe Wird Uns Abreißen

She is a form
fitting dress
you slip into
quite well. Give yourself some space, Assia, stretch out.
Gutman was a proper surname for you
at birth; you remain willful and fearless
in spite of her death.
She lingers, towering over
even the barbed wire curtains
of Nazi threat drawn over the horizons
of your youth. She is the only one
whose ambitions rode higher than yours,
with successes to match. Ted's devotion
to her is puzzling, when to you
crimes of passion are hardly
ticketable offenses anymore.

Your first husband did not exhibit such
clinginess. But that was a younger time,
with the two of you barely adults, back
in British Palestine, before the earth's face cracked
with age. That initial marriage,
Assia, it's the one that procured
your British citizenship. London in 1946
was a steep upgrade in living; your timing was never
flawed. Then you trafficked your heart
at the University of British Columbia, taking
a second husband. Could a Canadian
economist satisfy a woman of such grand
vision, though? Why, Canada barely had
an economy to speak of. Or, your needs
would far outstrip the coffers of such a nation.

Your recidivism continued. Everyone knows
you are a stunning beauty, Assia, but worst
of all so do you. And frontier folk
protecting their stock can attest that any
well-sprung mantrap needs two sides
of equal deadliness: your mind is sharpened
beyond reason, and your linguistic talents
could provide the foundation for literary
renown. In '56 you engage a third
husband, the poet David Wevill, a much younger
man, fomenting your terminal pattern. Marriage
is a formfitting poem you slide
well into. Is it growing a bit more
restrictive each time? Could it be
that you are expanding with age?

No! You remain breathtaking in every regard,
adhering to the Samurai philosophy
of leaving a beautiful corpse. Not one
to go halfway you intend to leave two
or three. This barbed wire curtain is
one of your own design, woven
meticulously over years, triple-
knotted at every turn. If you frequented
enough Chinese restaurants you would benefit
from the "Lovers in triangle not on square"
fortune cookie so many others gnaw on.
Maybe you abstain from those little almond
treats to preserve your figure.

Oriental philosophy be damned, Mr. and Mrs.
Wevill rent a flat from the poets Ted Hughes
and Sylvia Plath. Your heart and talent and goals
need not street-walk anymore, for in the Hugheses
you find not a rental but a home.
You slide between them more than snugly—

painfully, a birth in reverse, jamming
headfirst into a living thing
and compacting
down, smaller
and smaller,
before
you know
it, filling
their mold, not
the plaster tower
you hoped to build,
instead finishing their
basement, a cellar dweller
in their relationship. The affair
works in unanticipated fits of poor form…

You are outed.
You are impregnated.
The wife of your mark
gasses herself using an oven,
of all things. With younger men
it doesn't get this complicated, but
Ted has children, and a public life, like
the one you yearn for. Your translation of Yehuda
Amichai (with Hughes) goes unnoticed. He stows you
away in a rural cottage, shielded from public condemnation.
Worse even than the sudden invisibility is the onset of age, lost
beauty and prematurely graying hair, and not only serving
as nanny for Plath's boy and girl you endure aborting
the love child. Sylvia's knowledge seeps into your
mind, poisoning as would a slow leak,
her playing seer just before she died:

She wrote of "An illegitimate
baby" hidden in a drawer, its ugliness,
how it would become the knife

in your back. Its weight rides you,
parrot on your shoulder, repeating your groans
and complaints…but not your mistakes. It resides
in you with the overpowering gravity of a dead
star-born dream caving in on itself, black-holing
"what could have been." With each passing sunset
that Ted refuses to propose the light grows
dimmer, sucked into the hole, barbed wire curtains
three layers deep now. Wevill hasn't even
divorced you yet? Would that be a knife
in the back or the front? What about the knife down below
—the daughter you bear to Hughes, Shura.

And everywhere functionality forms
a vise clamping arteries shut…why,
this was her home! The rustic idyll Sylvia
was to experience with Hughes, their country
cottage! Populated with her children and friends,
decorated by her, still burdened with her
belongings. A child born late in life
accelerates your deterioration, as do Plath's spoons
and lingerie and mirrors. She is a black
shoe, one you know fails to fit, but you can live
within her—pale and white, a sun-evading troglodyte—
without fear. Ach du, ach du. Out in the storm
a wild orchid will perish. The hothouse is
your last resort. Can you marry it, marry it,
marionette your strings lead to her grave.

Where are your guts, man? These are
the consequences of your actions. Sylvia was
every bit the clairvoyant she claimed, as Ted
suspected, funneling her visions into her poetry
to a far greater extent than even he suspected.
She wrote not of herself but of you, the ghost
lingering after her death, contrary to common

belief. Consciousness is reduced to collaboration,
every action prescribed by your spectral parole
officer. Your existence is one of Plathtonic
relationship. The two of you could have achieved
monumental things together. You the worldly
older woman with experience taking her under
your wing, she the younger with many lifetimes
worth of intensity and the connections to make
your wings take flight. She left you
a flighty land-bound bird, long-necked cuckoo
with head stuck in the dirt, equipped with a survivaless
mind guaranteed for extinction.

You could have been the mother figure she craved,
statuesque and urbane; and like her mother Aurelia
Schober you are a German-speaking immigrant
who seduces married men, trapping them into nuptuals
of your own design. Sylvia must have recognized
the pattern after living with it strewn
over the windows of her girlhood home.
And like Aurelia you neglect your daughter,
instead focusing on your man's needs, wants.
Unlike young Sylvia your Shura has no grandparents
to escape to, developing into a woeful apparition
who leaves guests wondering if she has even been
taught speech. Your efforts at co-authoring
misery with Plath preclude all other effort.

Sylvia's fingers trail down the skin of your arms,
sliding over veins and tendons and knuckles,
nails sharper than your own, every touch and grip
guided by a symbiotic embrace more restrictive
than a plaster cast. Ted is distant,
roping family friend Brenda Hedden into a degrading
relationship. And that Carol Orchard, twenty
years his junior! How can you hope to compete with that?

And the magnifying glasses of guilt that are the eyes
of Sylvia's children, making you into the ant
trapped under a death-ray sun.
The Court Green halfway home is no longer
an option; you settle for house arrest
in London. With even less employability
than an ex-con you find your return
to work shuttered, barbed curtains drawn tight
by the bloody-handed gods of the advertising world.

Ted's patterns forgo the subtle stitching
of delicate fingers, opting instead for broad
strokes hammered out on the horizon's anvil,
such enormity both obvious and impossible
to get your mind around. He is setting up
a home with Carol the young nurse, playing
house and doctor and devil's advocate
sans advocacy. You are no longer ravishing
but ravaged. Shura, at four years of age, is
too small a vessel to ferry your hopes
to a new land. There is no avoiding prosecution
this time, no false identity to slither into…
the Lady Lazarus fund has been pilfered.

Sylvia's pattern, previously inscrutable
but embroidered with all the inescapability
of head-hanging despair, is clearly
in everything now. She inventoried in advance
your heart with the fervor of a
forensic pathologist, measured
and hemmed Ted's infidelity,
her needlework a vise
constraining arterial
flow. There exists no
loom in life broad
enough to encompass

Sylvia's weave,
Assia, you
know that
now.

She opened the door for you, Assia
Gutman Lipsey Wevill-not-Hughes,
she opened the oven door with kindness.
Finish the sentence.
Give Shura a dose of sleeping pills.
Pull her into the kitchen
on a mattress. Take the pills yourself,
with whiskey. Blow out the pilot light,
leave the oven running.
Lay down next to Ted's little girl,
that sad shadow of Sylvia's brighter duo.
Rest assured.
Rest assured that nobody will know,
or care. Even those close to Hughes
will not learn of your death
for months. Your passing is Plath
screaming into a void.

Double Indemnity

I

On setting out from the land of Myth, I wonder, Ted, if you would be so enthusiastic were you to be made aware of the trials ahead. It will be like this: your vessel is fine, all will agree on that point. And the sea will call…or could it be the beckoning of distant sirens, perhaps Leukosia lashed to the crags just as surely as countless souls are lashed to her voice. But just as the shark chases and consumes the skin and muscle and bone of his next meal, without seeking spirits or the sorrow of beings connected to said meal, so too does Leukosia not merit condemnation. She can only be what she is…very big of you to note that, Ted. If you encounter her on your voyage you can pass along that moral approval. Just don't expect the shark to swim away with an empty mouth after you pet it. Oh, of course you wouldn't. Such a thing would disappoint not just you, but your lady as well; she—the sea—will rock gently, but not with a promise to be so

II

You were always the dark horse, Ted, never what should be expected of the British literati: sprung from the farms of Mytholmroyd, a military man, dark and rugged in appearance; not bright or lofty but crushed by the future's unspeakable burden— or, the bodies dredged in its undertow. Being landlocked cursed you… how could you anticipate what the seas can do to a man? They carried women to your shores, deposited love and the promise of a bloodline among the kelp and ambergris and wreckage and who could turn away a goddess sprung from a clamshell? Refuse the pearls of wisdom she lavished you with, dark as squid ink on the papyrus of your soul? Nobody blames you. Any man would be considered as blessed under those circumstances. Knowing Sylvia only three or four months before being married at the church of St. George the Martyr Holborn was not a rush, it was an eternity waiting to unite with one so supreme. We will reserve judgment. Sylvia was a beauty with strong spirit, fierce wit, the sharp teeth of something primitive and inescapable. Yet somehow she was yours, or rather: you were hers. If anybody should recognize a goddess it was you, Ted, with your focus on anthropology studies at the university rivaling your accomplishments in the study of English. And what of Sylvia's study of you? The sheer terror of her eyes pre-dating every move, thought, scribble must have been maddening. Did that seed the need to direct Sylvia's writing with prompts and criticisms at every turn? Of

always. She will follow the
moon in its dark
lead. Danger,
always danger. The dirty
green of her eyes will swirl
around your craft, attuned to your
every move. Are you a god to deserve such
attention? A hero, at least, with a ship fashioned
from timbers of the Argo or the Arc? Or, on
your woman will you become a speck
adrift on her ever-changing
skin? Within every wave
will ride half-man,
half-fish
Tritons, perhaps
even more human than you.
Or, Leviathan shrugging tsunamis
into being, the friendly Nagas granting
wishes, none of those serpents disrupting your course.
Or, Nereus' daughters the sea nymphs at play:
Erato slowly rising tides like dough,
Glauke sprinkling shimmers upon
the water, Phersusa
kneading swimmers
against rocks with a wave
and a giggle. The Pahuanuiapitaaiterai
might wander from its native Tahiti to splash
just off the bow, taking an orca to the bloody depths
in its maw. On dry land sea gods are even worse
—remember the tale of Susanowo sealing his
sister the sun in a cave, allowing wild
spirits to roam free and terrorize
a dark world while his own
body of wind
and thunder destroyed
all in his path. Or, how Poseidon

course, she hung on your every word. Even more maddening, that must have been, to have somebody with the skill of a poet laureate at just the undergraduate level of her career placing such faith in you. You had age on her, though, and a mind that had never been institutionalized…dull the fear, that should, yes, quite. So you allowed her to watch, to gaze and graze in your shadow. it was a feat of Herculean magnitude to let her work and support you financially while you pursued a writing career, and her own career was put on life-support in the back room, walled in behind the nursery. Could you face the men of your time without a mask of self-hate? Face Sylvia without a plaster casting to smooth over the reality haunting your vision, while her eyes were crusted with barnacled dreams? Or perhaps she, too, saw the inequity, yes? That must be how you permitted the affair to happen. Assia Wevill materialized to fulfill a fantasy that was intended to keep the marriage afloat. You dutifully allowed for friendship, as it cleared the home for your writing sessions. Sylvia could not explain it all away, could she …lies sparkle with too much glare in the light of conversation. The reason historians rage in debate half a century later is like a two-backed monster with a name unrecognizable in your lexicon; the affair was not initiated by you or Assia, but by Plath herself. The shame must have hunted from the river to the streets, torching every shadow, bloodlust whirling out of control in its search for your soul's Alamo. Which path did you choose, to hide away from the world in grief's cavern, or to ride out and meet the beast on your warhorse? As you yourself wrote: "We didn't find her—

turned on his sister Demeter as she grieved her daughter Persephone, driving Demeter to disguise herself as a mare, and Poseidon himself took the form of a stallion to violently impregnate her. But as elemental forces the Gods are neither good nor bad, they merely are. Are we not fashioned in the image of the gods, Ted, is that your question? Danger, always danger in your reasoning. The sea will contain more than just green eyes, other pairs are bound to follow you, swelling blue or even gray. Sailing in silence you will take what bounty the sea offers, but your vision is doomed to drift to cliffs, somehow gracious, as if all a cove, secretly rubbing the idol of Nduthina in your pocket; all the way from Fiji he should grant clear passage and bountiful nets, but we'll keep his status as patron of adultery between us, eh? Will sea god Agwe whisper in your ear as well? He is just one of three husbands to the love goddess Erzulie. We are crafted in the image of our creators, you'll argue. Did not Ve, Vili, and Odin carve the first man and woman from two pieces of driftwood— not enough for making a raft— and there will be plenty of other bits of debris drifting on the tide; should they be left untouched? And, will you turn away from

she found us. She sniffed us out. She sat there slightly filthy with erotic mystery." Us, Ted. Despite your best efforts it was impossible to maintain that poker face forever, the mask of self-hate slipping. What possible compromise could be made by a couple in this position? If a goddess exhibits adulterous behavior, what is left for mortals other than to follow the lead. You loved Sylvia too well, Ted. Pursuit of her happiness led to a pair becoming a pair-and-a-half; your wife, for her part, added you to the decoupling, thinking the act along you wanted something more than her. But you went along with it, a single act the first mistake. Assia, Sylvia, and Ted adrift in the darkness of a bed, managing to stay afloat longer than they should have, perhaps. For one gifted with second sight your Sylvia failed to predict what would happen next: instead of she and Assia unleashing their collaborations on the world, astounding the literary establishment with the prowess of ex-Germanesses, you disrupted the ebb and flow of expectation with your gravity. The redistribution of Sylvia's love was enough to endure, but to then find yourself under siege by the love of another! The gods carved Assia in the form of a glamour model, another gift, one sacrificed to you by your very wife. Did you feel blessed? Cursed? Despite the unintentional nature of your crime did you feel guilty? Exhilarated? Assia was an even better match, perhaps, than the overreaching goddess who bore your children. Assia was perfectly mortal. Sylvia chronicled her self-the helpless fish appearing beside your vessel? You should. But on its gasping lips are the promise to save you in return for assisting it. It will fit into the empty brassiere below deck. "The Maruts are coming," the fish will warn you. "Head further into the cove. You'll find the mouth of a river awaiting you. Enter it with my blessing. Stay away from open water." Doing as it suggests you will look back out to sea and observe destruction manifest as wind demons tear through the water and batter themselves against the cliffs. Is that you making a clever escape or is it a disaster you triggered by leaving the ocean behind? The fish will grow, requiring new housing in a wine barrel. "Pay no mind to what you see inland," the fish will advise. "It is just a trick of the smoke and fog." And, sure enough, apparitions will wander past the river banks, more than merely terrifying, but themselves terrified, seeming lost and confused, wretched as they claw at their own faces, naked and abused. It will be easy to divert your gaze from such things. Bigger than a brassiere, than

induced downfall with "In Plaster," the duplication of herself detailed; a close-fitting, beautiful new one and an infirm original. At first the new desired the adoration of the original, then sought to commandeer everything in the original's life. "She wanted to leave me, she thought she was superior, and I'd been keeping her in the dark, and she was resentful...secretly she began to hope I'd die. Then she could cover my mouth and eyes, cover me entirely, and wear my painted face..." Hers was the tragedy of one who risked all, and lost even more; hubris of Greek proportions. From basking in your love, to Assia's love, to sitting just beyond the glow of your and Assia's love for each other as winter descended. Of Assia your wife went on, "I used to think we might make a go of it together—after all, it was a kind of marriage, being so close. Now I see it must be one or the other of us." None but the three of you stood witness to this knowledge, and soon enough Sylvia crossed herself off the witness list. Could your rejuvenating love affair with Assia survive the secret? She gave you shelter from the storm surrounding your wife's death. She kept your eyes off the scandalmongers, snatched their words from the air with her tongue. Like Plath Assia was an accomplished painter; the two of you had a pair of illustrated books in the works. Like Plath Assia was a skilled writer; your collaborative translation bore fruit, but the screenplay never saw the light of day. Like Plath Assia kept your love triangle to herself. Actually, Plath's silence was bought with death...there was the troublesome novel manuscript of hers, *Double Exposure*, and like "In Plaster" it described her life as a doppelgänger —only this time in much greater detail. In dangerous detail. For such a deformity to be a barrel, the fish will need to be tossed overboard. "Allow me," it will say, hooking a line from your ship on its horn, towing you along. When you wonder how the waters can remain so beautiful, so tranquil among wastelands your companion will burble, "This is Am-no-yasu-gawara!" And you will spring to life, recognizing this as the fabled river of Heaven. Swinging the cup of Mannanon Mac Lir you will seek to swallow paradise. But. At every turn murders of crows tear at the flesh of black creatures searching, searching, searching through decaying morsels for their prize. With water at your lips a new recognition will overtake you, Ted. Lethe, the river of forgetfulness spreads before you as you plow ahead, ever closer to losing yourself in its flow. You will dump the contents of the cup on the startled face of your "savior," wrestling your vessel free of the half-woman's clutches, knowing there is always a way out of Hades. Drawing closer to your woman the sea something will feel off. A sudden shallow, a sand bar, a rib of Jormagandr exposed and glistening under the stern

exposed, naked, abused, well it would destroy everything. *Double Exposure* vanished, along with key journals, out of deference to your children according to you. But your love child with Assia also vanished, in a doctor's clinic before it could ever be born. If ever your harbor were to be drained Ted we would find rotting a fleet never permitted to set sail. Such as the life you could have had with Assia: marriage, romance or even a career. It was all sacrificed in the effort to keep Sylvia alive. Expending the entirety of your next decade's effort focused on publishing Plath instead of pursuing your own writing career was not the act of somebody no longer in love, disengaged. Despite the daughter Assia bore you—innocent Shura—you shuttled them away to the shadows in order to preserve your mother's deteriorating health. It was clear your family could never be a home for Shura, so Assia, in seeking to spare your daughter consignment to an orphanage, made a note in her final days to "execute yourself and your little self efficiently." After the act the writing community closed ranks; no one spoke of the murder-suicide and it went unreported in the papers. Assia related to others that in bed you smelled "like a butcher," but the art community convinced itself your bouquet was that of a saint, a martyr. You knew the truth of it, maintaining a healthy distance from your mother for weeks. Your father and sister, they just could not keep their mouths sealed, could they? On revealing to your mother what happened to Shura your mother died of a stroke. Did your relationship with your sister and father perish too, or did you find it in yourself to forgive their loose lips? It was no mistake that "Blood Wedding" by Federico Garcia Lorca is among your sun's glare—always an exhibitionist, Loki's son. Climbing the rigging you will discover in the distance your woman receding, exposing every dead and dangerous thing she kept concealed on your behalf. She will allow no means of traversing the space between. Long gone are the blue eyes, the green eyes, the gray eyes. All that will remain are the black eyes that turn and stare, slowing time down to a torturer's pace, the black eyes belonging to the perfect kiss. Can you revert, set things back to the way they were, become a piece of driftwood awaiting divine discovery? Proteus would find that a trifling feat, but then he also possessed the power of precognition …as did the woman you left behind. But wood will avail you naught. It surrounds, frames you, taken with the rot of a beached whale too stubborn to die …Saint Ted going down with the ship.

body of translations. Your radio play *Difficulties of a Bridegroom* was not so much a callous last straw breaking Sylvia's back as it was your own shattered spine peeking through tough skin and mask. Still, life failed to break you. You managed the marriage vows once again. You returned to print with a slew of books, not the least of which absorbed ten years of effort, *Gaudete*, about a vicar in a remote locale being replaced by an elemental changeling, a creature who attempts to father a new messiah by mating with all the town's women. Is that what happened, Ted, did a double slip in and ruin your life, killable only with the sacrifice of your loved ones? Or was it a simple case of recreating what you had with Sylvia, or trying to, something so good it could not function in this world? Woman after woman, lie after lie. Controlling the publication of Plath's work with such ferocity protected not only her secret, but yours, a shape shifting feat that made it possible for you to become poet laureate of England on John Betjamin's death, because success always came at the cost of life for you. But you tied yourself to the mast and sang a lullaby for rats as they leapt into the seething red sea …Saint Ted going down (with the ship).

The Peculiar Case of Hannibal X

[taken from Rapipedia.org]

Name: Warwick Fray Barrington
Born: 4/24/74
Died: 2/16/11
Aliases: Alchemist, Cripblood Bitchslap the Seventeenth, First Power, Hannibal X, Unforgiven
Posse: Alien Nation, AKA "Hell-Drinking Beer-Raisers"
Tagging Name: H-X (pronounced "hex")

Personal History:

Barrington was raised in an area of southeast Washington, DC near the Navy Yards known for its high crime rates. The interracial child of a failed debutante and a mental patient, his family's resources were limited, disallowing the pursuit of higher education. Barrington's naturally copious intellect was instead left to corruption by street crime influence. Enduring multiple childhood sexual assaults did not improve his prospects, nor did the neglect and abuse he encountered at home. His suicidal father was too preoccupied with his own clinical depression to protect young Warwick from the Münchausen Syndrome By Proxy inflicted on him by his own mother. A definitive sociopath, Barrington could not be considered to develop "friendships;" however, he did cultivate a close-knit group that may or may not have been a gang and/or "satanic cult." They were known on the street as the Alien Nation, with individual members referred to as Hell-Drinking Beer-Raisers. All known associates of this group are now deceased, the bulk of them passing away during a prolonged stint Barrington served in a psychiatric care facility. Having spent his 20s under 24-hour supervision Barrington tried to assimilate into society at age 31. He held a number of minimum wage jobs and led a relatively normal life until, at age 36, he decided to end it all.

The Revenge:

In what has become considered the "rock opera" of horrorcore rap Barrington performed a piece titled "The Revenge" live over the InterWeb while holding seven people hostage. The hostages—all employees of Eastern Shore Remodeling & Contracting—were slain one by one during the performance. Despite the fact that escape was assured Barrington chose to take his own life before the cameras, maintaining his "artistic integrity" given the theme of his performance. A transcript of the rap he performed follows; its ramifications will be covered in the Cultural Impact section.

"The Revenge"
by Hannibal X

That's right, it's the Hell-Drinking Beer-Raiser Hannibal X, the Unforgiven Alchemist arithmetic called the First Power with the sixth sense, wettin' it up from the seventh seal to the ninth gate…rugged and stylish for 2011… this one goes out to all ya'll sleazaks, ya know who ya are up in this muth-aaaaaaaaaaaaaaa!

It's the Alchemist hittin' ya wit da alchefist dropping spiritual Alkaseltzer on your secular bomb shelters so bear witness you don't possess enough infernal fitness to hear this and survive the demonic got unionized to negotiate wages of sin 'cause we workin' overtime so don't come around with your whinin' and cryin' the First Power will touch ya like your name's Lou Diamond I'm domiciled in the Alien Nation in flagrant violation of restricted migration known as the terroristic sound sensation this threat level goes up to eleven 'cause H-X threatens from Hell to Heaven serial murder like Se7en was romantic comedy driven drivel your liver I will dribble on the Supreme Court and make a slam dunk in the Sixth Justice's junk when it comes to bloodsport the Unforgiven is professional nine rounds in the draft doin' ya in the confessional with a gat and if you don't worship Satan I'll hit ya with a black cat skinned more than one way still alive with claws in your arterial spray sinkin' in fangs like body parts in Chesapeake Bay and don't let me see your girl H-X's bed is known as silent hill even if your daughter's on the pill I drop 212-degree sperm boiled alive from inside I'll stay all up in her internal eternal blowin' on that fallopian tuba creatin' a scream symphony murda chamber choir pain is what you acquire if you wear the wrong attire if you don't know Alien Nation colors it's a tire 'round your waist filled with gasoline and fire see our colors can't be put on and taken off ya only see 'em with the outer layer gets lost to the flayer see if ya can still be a player rockin' that subcutaneous fat if you're a sleazak my crotch is where it's at almost time ta cut my veins but stll got a couple plays left ta cause da end of days and just like Mormons got spiritual babies I got infernal infants listen to them tiny cloven feet pitter-patter I got more blood splatter than Dexter don't bring your sleazak around cause I'll vex her body parts her soul and her heart's desire abortion is what I'll buy her when it comes to her pubes it's deforestation this is Alien Nation of which H-X is the boss all other cliques operate at a loss defenestration is their only option straight up bakin' 'em roundin' up they illegitimate children in a burning buildin' let 'em fight it out with a razorwire chitterlin' and the winner gets out alive…'til I throw 'em back in but H-X will never be captured because he leaves the law fractured with his hairy testicular stature got some poison meth manufactured in the elephant man's cranium spreading more toxic shit than if salmonella was in Sarah Palin they wanna get high but I taint 'em corpse gray is what I paint 'em with some Chuck Wagon I bait 'em dump they body in the Ganges for some gators and sharks to tear apart no chance from the start do not pass go ya don't wanna know why they call me Hannibal don't talk that Chuck Wagon ramble I'll wipe your junk with a bramble don't want to be another head on my mantle get down and pray 'cause I'm the sangre santo don't care 'bout no: northside, eastside, southside, westside, H-X claims all six sides of the pentangle pentagram with a more expensive war program than tax dollars in the Pentagon with more sidearms than Vietnam if this is a talent show I'm bangin' a gong like I'm bangin' your skull in the middle of the precinct or the middle of the mall harder than Lucifer you will fall into the burning pit barbecue out back ya sleazak yeah H-X is the suicidalist so cancel your bridal list 'cause your sleazak is just grist in the mill on haunted hill behind my fortress if ya enjoy salad then toss this see you're comin' on like you're so fast and you're furious but when you look at me ya know you're gettin' bi-curious so get back in the closet where ya know the skirt is the construction site is where the dirt is amputation got your blood spurted lookin' at your sleazak got me perverted lookin' at me even your moms and pops flirted so they also had to get dirted this kind of evil makes God hurted an admonishment is harshly worded but atonement just ain't worth it and like a deep-fried pterodactyl ya got birded I skeet from your sheets to your feet to my heat rockin a 4/4 beat on your head with a hammer I'll take your sleazak and damn her damage her cut a hole in her thigh and slam her straight up derange her like a cyst I will drain her upside-down drawn and quartered another serial killing being reported another serial drilling in her carotid artery and her bags done been ported to Hell's honeymoon suite with a waterbed filled with blood and a whore's head or two or three or even more than you can count so don't try to sort 'em out got more hits than Tekken steady chuggin' on that Kraken black rum performing redrum burn down your crib and build a slum filled with zombie necro demons your IQ is dumb so in your bum is where ya can stick your thumb and suck it put your head over a bucket then I chop it Haitian style and drop-kick it when your blood is clotted I can take a lick gettin' cannibalistic sick makin' you into a necro trick the 8mm porno flick sequel Alien Nation Part 6: The Revenge and I'm wreckin' more beds than the Entity got requiems for more dreams than Freddy killin' more environments than BP and Getty if your wife's Indian she'll commit suttee when I put your body in the trunk of the Chevy and drive that American-made into the levy drinkin' whiskey and rye add some Hennessy silly little wannabe wants to step to me but gets turned into some organic gardening rollin' with that Satanic chemistry it's called some ding-dang alchemy pimpin' out more diablerie than the entire Donner Party and their extended family punk you can't see through me but I'll put a hole in you so I can peep on your sleazak droppin' her panties and takin' a shower like in a slasher movie the mask is ski the perp is me guzzle blood like coffee add my own cream to your sleazak's kidneys deviant sex therapy abstinence scares me Heaven stares me down or tries to but gets meek the blade is sleek from my white meat to my dark meat and that's the end of my heartbeat

Cultural Impact:

The ramifications of "The Revenge" were both multifaceted and multi-staged, playing out over a number of years. Predictable, of course, was the mitigated mental healthcare reform pushed through state legislatures across the United States, as well as the media backlash against hip hop culture in general, and rap in particular. Barrington also became a folk hero among criminal elements and the disenfranchised. Other cultural ripples include:

*Establishment of the Clean North style, of which Barrington is assumed to be the progenitor (this is a matter of mild dispute, as witnesses claim to remember all Alien Nation members using this style). Clean North references a fashion aestethic as opposed to musical dynamics or lyrical content/delivery. See the seperate "Clean North" entry for more details.

*Kraken Rum Company reported a 28% increase in revenue after the incident, despite having their products banned in Virginia, Maryland, and the District of Columbia.

*In the world of hip hop rap changed drastically, as a new set of laws required all threats of violence in rap lyrics to be followed up by detention, an official inquiry, and a psychiatric evaluation. Many performers opted to alter the content of their rhymes rather than "get hit with a H-X" for each infraction—which could amount to upwards of one hundred per album—and the resulting two to four weeks out of action each infraction entailed. Horrorcore rap, much like the "extreme" pornography of the 1970s, continues to exist only on the InterWeb, in the black market, and in rogue nations.

*Strict oversight and regulation of sales practices by home remodeling companies was enacted first in the Mid-Atlantic region, then on a national scale. The number of remodelling-related police reports have now dropped to an all-time low.

*A group calling themselves "St. Bruno's Martyrs Brigade" has recently orchestrated a series of criminal horrorcore rap spectacles engineered to result in the performer's death, and that of many others. See their separate entry for more details; a good portion of this has to do with the following "Savior" section.

The Revenge Part II: Empirical Proof

At 19:00 hours on August 14, 2011 there was an inexplicable worldwide occurance that can only be described as "occult." From people playing simple games of Oijia to published horrorscopes to palm readings to deep space transmissions…a follow-up rap was received. Accurate translations were independantly confirmed in fifty-three languages, from over twelve thousand sources worldwide. Debate continues to rage between "believers" and "disbelievers" as regards the supernatural, particularly due to the fact that any and all parties are loathe to embrace the second purported Barrington rap as proof of an afterlife. Regardless, Alien Nation cells have sprung up in every population center around the globe, acquiring more adherents with each passing day. An International HDBR Task Force has been created to monitor the activities of these cells…

[discussion continued at Rapipedia.org]

SuiPsalms

I'm a dead man in a dead land being stroked by a red hand
In the dark something is falling apart…one thing's for sure: it's gone too far
It could be the smell or it could be my hell or it could be that maybe I just can't tell
It could be the grief or it could be the scream or worst of all it could just be me

>   Soothe me with a suisong
>   Lullaby me…it won't take long
>   Sentence me with a suipsalm
>   Lament me…it won't take long

My inner child is leaking bile from an ulcerated smile
Dissolving my resolve and making me wild
With dissolute fear that he can hear the song suicidal
And we're morally bankrupt so we jump truth's turnstile
Without even a quarter of the remorse that could fill a crack vial
If Heaven is mental candy I'm on a sugar-free diet
Because karma is a vending machine full of matches and gasoline

>   Soothe me with a suisong
>   Lullaby me…it won't take long
>   Sentence me with a suipsalm
>   Lament me…it won't take long

It's dangerous to know what danger is
And the kindness of a medicated fist
And you don't know me yet and you don't know me now
Don't know me and you sure don't want to find out
And I want to break out and I want to sneak out
To steal the scream from Cleopatra's mouth

I'm drinking my life like whiskey and rye
I'm gorging on truth and spitting up lies
To tell you the truth I'm sick of you
To tell you a lie you're really quite nice
I'm drinking my life like whiskey and rye
I'm gorging on truth and spitting up lies
To tell you the truth I'm sick of me
To tell you a lie we are what we bleed

> Soothe me with a suisong
> Lullaby me…it won't take long
> Sentence me with a suipsalm
> Lament me…it won't take long

2 Corinthians 5:2 Meanwhile we groan, longing to be clothed with our heavenly dwelling…

2 Corinthians 5:8 We are confident, I say, and would prefer to be away from the body and at home with the Lord.

Off the Chain and Down the Drain

i held the Yucatan in the palm of my hand
and i said this is surreal
i sold it all to the man in the stall
and he asked me how did i feel
better i lied and diverted my eyes
when i heard the water flush
the horrors we contrived and all the wasted lives
came to me in a rush

so i went down south with gold in my mouth
and lead in my hand
without the slither of a doubt i remained devout
and burned the land
the structure of morality collapsed and splashed
in a seething sin-quake
we were trapped plundering a paradise
we could never take

god does despise
april and so do i
there is no worth on heaven or earth
yet we continue to deny
(x2)

the trippy majesty of a book-born disease
made me right
sweet curses melted on my tongue nourishing
divine blight
the blood-washed colors cleansed my eyes
with smokey disabuse
starving for truth i found in you
the virtue of a noose

god does despise
april and so do i
there is no worth on heaven or earth
yet we continue to deny
(x 4)

Deus Irate

I am your new disease
Don't penicillin me
I'm in your bloodstream
Racing…straight to your heart
We'll share another scream
Together in misery
This romantic surgery
Nothing…can cut us apart

Sometimes love is the fire
consuming everything but your rage
Sometimes love is the water
washing away everything but your pain
Sometimes love is the blade on your wrist
and the mirror revealing your shame
And sometimes love strips your identity
a crumbling headstone with no name

Sometimes hate is the mortar
mending everything but your resolve
Sometimes hate is the water
leaving you christened but not absolved
Sometimes hate is the fire
leaving you scalded but not dissolved
And sometimes hate becomes your identity
a headstone with no name at all

I am your new disease
Don't penicillin me
I'm in your bloodstream
Racing…straight to your heart
We'll share another scream
Together in misery

This romantic surgery
Nothing…can cut us apart

Sometimes death is a chance
for the life you always wanted
Sometimes death is the answer
to the question you've always hunted
Sometimes death is the success
you lost but remain haunted
And sometimes death is no more
than your dreams malnourished and stunted

I am your new disease
Don't penicillin me
I'm in your bloodstream
Racing…straight to your heart
We'll share another scream
Together in misery
This romantic surgery
Nothing…can cut us apart

Death By Disobedience

1
They was all told
the same: strip them
clothes off, get down
on the floor, crawl
like a motherfucker.

Now, me and the boys been
doing this sort of thing for
years. We got it down.
You stand over them
with trained attack

dogs, "dissuasion spray"
dispensers, cattle prods.
Put your boots to use
before them other things,
'cause boots ain't expensive

when you compare them.
The warden gets upset
if the workers—you know,
the prisoners—are too busted
up to make shirts the next

day. So we bust them up just
enough. Anybody puts up
a ruckus gets it put to them hard
…plus we can say they're gang
members; that means you can

put them in solitary forever
if you want. If he got

a busted leg or arm or whatever
that don't make no difference.
Put his ass in convulsions
for a few hours. Wouldn't be
no use in the factory wing
of the penn anyhows. Dogs got
to be put to work if they
got any hope of staying

sharp. Every couple days or so
is fine; overdo it and you wear
the poor K-9s out. Once in a black
and blue moon a con kicks it,
on tape no less. See, regs state

correctional officers got to record
all actions taken against the population
to show it ain't no "improprieties"
going down. One of us boys misses
out and stands at the back to record.

Coroner rules them deaths
suicides. Why would you
put up a fight when
you know what's
gonna happen?

2
Carrianne watched Jules die
yesterday. He wouldn't calm down
over by the school store; she was
in line buying a candy bar and
saw it all. Some of those special
education types can't handle being
out in the real world where people
aren't paid to hold your hand all

day long, not even when they're 16.
Nobody knows why he was
so upset but the cellphone
his parents gave him for
emergencies was missing and
the police said it got used a bunch
of times last night and they found
it in a dumpster this morning and
they'd like to talk to anybody
who knows anything about that,
but Carrianne isn't convinced
that means anything. Retards lose
track of stuff all the time.
Mr. Gussey, the security dude, he
tried reasonably yelling at Jules
to calm down. But he wouldn't.
When Jules knocked Reb's tray
of food on the floor Mr. Gussey got
scared for folks' bodily safety and
whatnot, so he had to stun gun Jules.
But it hit him in the eye because
Mr. Gussey doesn't tell people
about this but he's got a glass eye
—Carrianne saw him cleaning it one
time when he had her locked in
the security office and he didn't
think she could see what he was up
to. So maybe he can't tell how far
things are sometimes; that's not his
fault. Anywho, the eye exploded and
Jules was on the floor shaking around
all over bumping into people's things
and spilling their drinks and stuff started
coming out of his pants—from down there
—and it all smelled so horrible and
was so scary, and she had to take even

more Ambien than usual to sleep last
night. Why couldn't Jules just try to act
normal for once? Is being special worth
being dead? He didn't have to make
her see that. Her mother already booked
counseling sessions during her
usual shopping time, and they cost
so much Carrianne won't be getting
that handbag she wanted this season.
The newspaper said the coroner said
Jules died of "excited delirium" but
they didn't say what that meant. She
figures he kept a stash in his locker
and liked to party between classes,
but the papers didn't have the balls
to come out with it because of his
family and all. Also his exploding
eye didn't have to do with "his
cause of death" either.
Tommy slides in step with her
on the way to Spanish 3, that famous
—around school, anyway—sexy
glimmer in his eye, leaning
in close to whisper, "Heard you
saw what happened yesterday."
She nods in the affirmative, so
he continues, nearer and huskier,
"Wasn't the first time that spaz
pissed or shit himself."
"That's so mean!" she says
unable to restrain
her smile.

3
The women could almost be
pretty, if they got makeup, washed up,

or put on women's clothes—not socialist
uni-gender garbage—and didn't stretch their
faces out in such angry, ugly
shapes. This one especially sticks
out, kind of delicate looking, dressed
like maybe she could have an office
job if she wanted. There's something
extra behind her eyes, too, some
secret worth cracking her open
to get at. But she's angry and twisted
up as any of them you're going to
find here. Adult children who should
know better. Anarchists who don't believe
in God or banks or the rulership
of law. And they dare to stand
in the shadow of the financial district,
where my older brother died a hero working
to his last breath to save liberty from
the Muslim-world's jaws. He and the EMTs
he worked with, unable to escape the tower's
collapse. How can so many people want to spit
on all those sacrifices? It's like
the Captain said at briefing: this is
an organized assault on our nation's
promise that citizens can pursue
the right to work or sell goods. And what's
our job? That's right, boys: we stop
assaults. Some of them carry signs accusing
me and the guys of "infiltrating" their
"peaceful gathering" and doing things
to cause them to get arrested, but I know
for a fact that's not the case; we got orders
to do the opposite, on account of nobody
behind the blue line wants to take down
a brother in arms. We have to keep it clear who's
who in all this craziness, because it's us

against them, and that's not something
that was ever our call. One or two jump the Freedom
of Speech barriers we erected to protect
their rights and all, and they get taken
down just the way they want. Their homies are
sitting around pulling on the bong, watching
TV and pointing saying "Hey, lookit! He did
it! He's the man!" And they're booing
and dropping a deuce on me and the guys, the ones
who put it on the line every single day saving
their mothers and kids from screw-ups not too
different from them. And it's smart, I'll give
them that, using a bunch of chicks too,
chicks that will look fuckable to Jews, because
that'll guarantee they get on TV and all. Pictures
in the paper. Look at us ugly cops picking
on the chick you'd buy as a slave if this
was back in the Biblical days. Got God on my
mind because my boy's Godfather just got laid
off when his boss' investment money disappeared,
and the queer boy waving a sign on me
and the guys, so close you know he's trying
to get us to smack him one upside the head, and
it says: Jesus said "Watch out! Be on your
guard against all kinds of greed; a man's
life does not appear in the abundance
of his possessions. Truly, I say unto
you, it will be hard for a rich
man to enter the kingdom of
Heaven. You cannot serve
both God and…"
yada yada, some other socialist crap. Jesus
never said that, He said "You cannot
strengthen the weak by weakening the strong."
He also said wash your ass and get a job
if you don't want to make a public park

stink like the zoo. And the men and boys,
dropouts I'm guessing, some of them are
dilated like a mother, and some are pumping
fists in the air and screaming like they just shot
a load in Hitler's slit throat, and others look
like monkeys in cages angry because they're
confused and too stupid to figure it all out on
their own. And just what the hell are they
so angry about? Don't they know how this
all ends? Something different goes down,
I wasn't looking but now one of the white
collars down here to make sure us blue collars
don't screw it all up, he walks over
to the penned-in group in response to whatever
it was. And he sprays them with pepper
spray? Empties the whole thing? On like a
dozen? Something inside sends up a warning
flag and I almost tell the guys I've got
to take a call with the plan of coming back
a minute later to say I've gotta go because my
boy is in the hospital, but I don't. The guys need
me. My brother didn't turn and leave, not
even when the world was blowing up around
him. The one chick, the delicate raging office
type, she got the worst of it because she was up
front. When the crowd pushes back and the barrier
goes down, she's knocked forward along with
it. Me and the guys move in to get this back
under control. Two of us grab her blind and
screaming, drag her to the side, try to
subdue her without getting Porky's spray
all over us. That's what we call him:
Porky. White collar, silver-spoon-fed
wannabe fatso who doesn't know street
cred from a squirrel's fudge tunnel,
so he does everything he can to live

up to the stereotypes. Donuts. Fake
Irish accent. Before we can thank
Porky for the gift the buttons on
this broad's shirt rip out from all
her resisting arrest. Colón yells
"Weapon!" and the guys' hands move
to her neck, arms bending into the
lateral vascular neck restraint.
McGawley is too big or she's too
small and when she tries to run
for it she turns in his grip
and now it's a choke hold, or
maybe he just doesn't know
how to do it right. I try
yelling but some idiot beams
a full Venti Latte off my
head and now I'm yelling
for a different reason,
just keeping the wolves
at bay, trying to block
out the scalding, and no I'm
not really going to start
spraying into a crowd but
they don't know that. By
the time I get myself
together the chick is
face-up on the pavement,
red as a boiled injun,
seizing like I don't know what.
The guys are looking at each
other like one of them should
know what to do, so Colón kicks
at her and orders her to stop. She
doesn't. The hippies are going apeshit.
Lucky for us a crowd dispersement unit hits
the scene. The chick, she's not even a woman

really. My little sister who just got out of
college is older. This is a girl. She's not
moving, and we have to explain why. She had
one of those "pretender" stun guns designed
to look like pink cellphones. Or, Colón thought
she did. It turned out to be just a pink cellphone.
He gave his cousin one after three guys tried to
force her into a car. The hippy chick, she never
saw us. All she knew was a bunch of men blinded
her and started grabbing her chest and legs
and arms telling her to be a good girl and
stop fighting or else we'd have to really
get rough. It's a good thing for us she
didn't have one of those pretenders,
except now that she's dead it's not
a good thing. Colón, he's already
got that flap in the press last year
hanging over his head. The guys make it
clear somebody like me should be the one
who made the weapons call. A guy like me
has a squeaky clean record, they say. A guy
like me has a wife and kid to think about.
A guy like me shouldn't have to worry about
his pension or jail time or worse. Me and
Sheryl, we're going to settlement next week.
Or first mortgage. Nothing is going to
mess that up. If this hippy chick
didn't want it she wouldn't have been
there. It's just, Sheryl…if she was standing here
with me she'd slap the shit out of my head. And
if she was standing there when Porky sprayed
the chick, if Sheryl was by my side I'd have
been slapping the shit out of Porky's head. But
she wasn't, and she isn't, and I make sure our
settlement's going to go just fine. The guys
let me know they'll be lining up to

take one for me whenever I need it in
the future. They're good like that. It
comes down I'll just get the slap-
on-the-wrist-treatment, we all will,
because each of us was involved "in
separate aspects of the incident." But still.
When I'm laying in bed that chick is
there under me, puffy and red and flapping around
trying to breath, trying to reach in her
beaded handbag for the asthma inhaler we
didn't know she had. And when I'm at my boy's little
league game my shoulders hunch down with the weight
because she's right there in the stands on
top of me, smelling like lavender and
spice and it makes me so angry because its
unfair. It's not on me, not really,
not on any of the guys.
Why did she have to be so angry? Why
couldn't she go home? Why did she have
to keep going even when she knew it
could only end badly?

4
If you don't cover your debts
be ready to pay the price.

There's no such thing as a free
ride. Not paying your way is
the same as sucking on a bullet.

When millions of homeowners
find themselves foreclosed on
there are fewer sofas to sleep
on, and they're all filled up.

When you're homeless you die

twenty years younger than every
one else. When you're homeless
you have chronic disease, sleep
deprivation, and nutritional
deficiency. Half of the adult
street population will die violently.

When you're a CEO you hire executive
protection to the tune of $70,000
per guard. They tend to be moonlighting
or retired police, and they handle
the riffraff nicely. You receive
$10 million even while losing your
bank $14 billion that year; bailouts
have their benefits. Your Tribeca
town home would cost over $22 million,
but it comes with having the job.

There's no such thing as a free
ride. Not paying your way is
the same as sucking on a bullet.

If you don't cover your debts
be ready to pay the price.

5
You survive two tours in Iraq,
come home to your wife and child,
work hard. Own three guns and body
armor, like many veterans…and

average citizens. You lay in bed
thinking how lucky you are not to be
messed up in all the trouble some
of your family got into. You cuddle

with your wife. Then there's yelling
outside your home, the front door
explodes in, men with automatic
weapons and armor pour in; the dead

relatives recently killed by home
invaders come to mind. You hide
your family in the closet, grab a gun,
step into the hallway to confront

whoever it is. You are shot almost 100
times. It is the police, performing
a drug raid. Although you have no drugs
you do have a chance of surviving

...maybe. Except paramedics are barred
from entering your home for an hour.
As the seconds tick away and your blood
escapes its housing you are not

comforted by your family, who are instead
detained outside, but even though you never
fired a shot you know they survived.
And other citizens should think

twice before exercising their right
to bear arms to defend themselves.
You don't raise a gun when people
who may be police officers attack.

6
Have you signed
up for the cleaning
crew? Or are you
with the
terrorists?

The Appalling Intricacies of Hexagons

A cornflower's merciless expanse marred by ivory cataracts, illumination flitting and gliding across, across, compelled by the force of a child with a golden stone skipped on the river overhead and breaking its surface with impetuous determination. Blue virgin no more for this shimmering penetration, this thoughtless intrusion pressing between the veils hanging overhead. It rests on humanity with all the weight of a mausoleum, all the protection of a wax house. The veils are growing gray with age, soon to run black. Air slowly ruptures free from the lungs of the collective dead, swarming angry and circulating through nature's beautiful ruins, stirring leafy columns of enough variety and splendor to stitch Roman eyes closed with phallic envy. Not the icy granite and marble of polished resting places, but the thorny precariousness of life.

The maternity ward is sterile, secure, full of
cubby holes to wall mothers in, wall in babies.
False notes in the highest octaves bashed out by
the awkward hand of a dilettante player: the hospital
administrator allows jargon to tumble from her
mouth in a steady stream, making the tour
for expecting parents more difficult than necessary.
Mia stalks among them solo, cradling her first
trimester belly and wishing it felt less extrinsic,
less artificial. The birthing suites boast the latest
in technological advancements and retractable
surgical lights over the beds and incubators
at the ready and Mia's head becomes a roulette
wheel, always landing on black. One couple in
particular raises a number of questions about safety
protocols, so Mia is spared the spotlight, neither Asian-
Americans or unwed mothers being abnormal in the big
city, and it strikes no one as odd, then, when
she inquires about intruder-related procedures.
Each potential life-consumer is bequeathed

with a bag of free samples brochures maps guides
advice all graven with images of smiling w/omen
holding infants, admiration/envy dripping
from the background onlookers.

Parents all too often rely on their children
as conversation crutches, magnets for attracting
ferrous-oxide-coated wrecks from the recreation
area's depths, at least in Mia's experience, not
unlike the bachelor who lays in wait with an
adorable dog on a leash. Occasionally the statistical white
buffalo emerges from the herd: an eligible bachelor
with an infant or toddler on a leash. Mia observes
him for a while with clinical detachment, circles
multiple times, bumps into him as would a shark
examining a questionable source of nourishment.
Mia: "Oh, excuse me! I'm terribly sorry about that."
    Jermane: "Not a problem…"
Mia: "Mia."
    Jermane: "Mia. Not a problem, Mia. It was probably just fate."
Mia: "Fate. You believe in fate…"
    Jermane: "Jermane. And yes I do. Fate blessed me with this
    beautiful day, and this beautiful daughter. Marlene."
Mia crouching to stroller height, tickling the baby's nose: "Oh! What a cutie-pie! How about a song?"

Babbity bouster Bumble Bee!
Fill up your bags, bring them to me!
Humming and sighing—with lazy wing
Where are you flying—what song do you sing?

'Who'll buy me honey pots? Buy Them? Who'll buy?
Sweet heather honey—come weigh them and try!
Honey bag, honey pot, home came she!
Nobody buys from a big bumble bee.'

Marlene smiles and Mia smiles so Jermane
smiles, their teeth dominos of happiness, a tumbling
effect spiraling throughout their bodies
lending to flesh and bone a buoyancy surpassing
that of mere air.
    Jermane: "You have a beautiful…singing voice."
Mia: "I have a lot of practice singing to babies."
    Jermane: "Know any other lullabies?"
Mia: "Maybe I can sing them for Marlene some day, if you'll let me."
    Jermane stepping forward, arm around Mia: "I call her Mouse."

The following day is lost to investigating
another possible source. The natural birthing
center is a benign growth in comparison to
the hospital's thrashing deformity flopping
on the horizon, vestigial limbs pinned down
by Gulliver's architects, drones buzzing with
effort to add new combs to the hive mind. *What
medications are you on, ma'am*: omega-3, vitamin
E, folic acid, bee pollen, magnesium, thiamin,
zinc, all in higher than recommended doses.
Strangely the tour group is as large as that for
the hospital's maternity wing; however unlikely,
none notice when Mia's prosthetic pregnancy
belly slips and has to be ratcheted tight. Pastel
colors and granola-crunching decor devour
fear—intact and screaming—in the unhinged jaw
that poses as a lobby. Nurse 4 is a slattern with cyprian
lips jade eyes a Stage-2 trull in her heart and she
will make out/off with one of the husbands on
this tour; Mia knows this, because the w/oman
watches the men the way she herself watches babies.
She exits before nurse 4 can recognize that selfsame
criminal flesh-greed and sound the klaxon,
exhorting the workers to swarm and defend this cluster.

The next encounter with Jermane is an affair of escalation. The afternoon is spent performing for Jermane and Marlene/Mouse, demonstrating what a good mother she would be, selling what a good wife she would be, peddling her quality as a playmate. Their apartment is the garden variety, not one of the poured concrete hive monstrosities she herself prefers. It is littered with mismatched decor struggling to convey a sense of quaint homeyness, a tattered veneer hastily slapped over the gaping hole left by a lack of female presence. Undoubtedly for Mouse's sake, that, to engender some sense of an unsundered home. Mia is thankful for the distraction of Jermane's own song and dance to mask shortcomings, as it prevents him from noticing her own. In fact it serves as an "in" for her…clearly he lacks confidence as regards homemaking. She begins in the kitchen, regurgitating the sweet honey of helpful critique. This would make cooking so much easier, and that would keep Mouse's feeding from involving a floor scrub, et cetera. And, only organic foods are allowed to infiltrate Mia's presence.

    Jermane: "Health nut, huh?"

Mia: "Don't you know a third of our food comes from pollinators, and they're being wiped out by all the chemical pesticides we use?"

    Jermane: ruminating on it briefly, before nodding and saying,

    "What the heck, it'll be good for Mouse."

The bulk of his goods are thrown away. She sinks her soul into him with all the desperation of a tiger bent on survival as it clamps down and bleeds a water buffalo to defenselessness.

The enormity of the cornflower is maddening, stretching from horizon to horizon, as is the sickly sweet stench of its decay. With a bloodshot blink the cataracts run red, the communal rage seeping, festering, composting under the compression of a shrinking world. Such is the dwelling place

of—and the compassion of—a God who hurts you as the world does bodies. The limitless suffering that is creation contracts, no longer content at playing mausoleum but desiring to cling to humanity's virtue as coffins cling to single-use suits, as splintered thrones cling to queens, as cells cling to bees, as honey clings to cells. Light bleeds through the cracks, spreads over surfaces with the efficiency of arterial spray. The prayers and hopes and dreams of untold multitudes filter up through the graying fishnet to provide kindling for that incensed pyre as it sways through the heavens with a hypnotist's precision.

Mia's fingertips trail over her scars, interpreting the braille of her agony. She assures herself it does not have to be that way again. The cycle is broken this time; attempting her death is needless now that she has scared up Jermane and Mouse. Besides, she reasons, her strength lies not in taking life out of this world but in bringing life forth. Jermane can never know of her femininity's malformation, what the doctors and specialists quite abstractly explain is an embryogenetic failure in the fusion of the Müllerian ducts. More technically termed and deceptively elegant: didelphys. Hers is the most exquisite didelphys they have encountered, rendering her the bearer of twins…double vagina, double cervix, double uterus, each with only one fallopian arm. How many deaths have those twins caused? Self-terminating pregnancy, the doctors tell her, hesitation in their words inspired by sympathy, or so they tell themselves, although the true cause is plain to Mia: disgust. The noose, the blade, the pills, the car. They all failed her. But Jermane, Jermane, Jermane and Mouse…it is a pity they cannot know of all the live births she has assisted in., of all those lucky w/omen.

At the park the three of them exist as if

coated in the thick tempera colors of Renaissance
masters. *The Last Lunch*, circa 2010. While
Mia and Mouse lose themselves in skylarking
Jermane purchases ice cream from the vendor
nearby, lemon and liquorice.
A man approaches Jermane: inquisitive, overly-familiar with the subject
of Mia.
    Jermane: not interested in whatever this fool is selling.
The man: "Whatever. When you're ready to get abstinent and sober look
up SA. Saved my life."
    Jermane: nonplussed to the point of subtraction, because although
    he knows he wasn't the one to deflower her, he cannot endure
    envisioning the depravity the stranger suggested Mia capable of.
Eyeing Jermane eyeing them, Mia does her
best to stay engaged with Mouse but misses
a step, discerning a subtle shift in the atmosphere.
Has some portion of her costume slipped?
The anatomy of benevolence is alien to her,
rending a tear in normalcy impossible to detect.
Or has a clue come to him via other means?

When she is confined to bedrest he does not delve into the why, press
past her discomfort or his own, instead settling on admonishments.
    Jermane: "Is this how you spend your free time?"
Mia: struggling to piece the words together: "Only when I'm not feeling
well."
    Jermane: "You do realize you're gonna turn into a chubby if you
    keep this up, right?"
Mia: "Why don't you come exercise me, then?"
She claws back the covers, but lacks the strength
to undo her undergarments. No matter; he
understands and supplies that service. Yellow
has bled into her visage…a sign of renal
derangement correlating to the didelphys? In
addition to the problems arising from her lack
of degenerated endometrial septae partitions,

the specialists had warned her of potential
kidney deformity and malfunction. They had run
tests, but…circumstances arose that prevented
her checking back in with the doctors. Ever.

     Jermane: "You sure, baby? Don't look so good."
They always ask, but they plow on ahead
regardless. The men never dive deep enough
to dislodge the vivisectionist slumbering within
Mia, are unable to drive their stakes through
the heart of the tormentor residing in the space
intended for her progeny. She is the crumbling
hospital teetering on the horizon, just concealed
by a tree line, whose rusted water tower inspires
silent thanks for health codes with each accidental
glimpse. Her maternity ward is piled high with
crumbled asbestos and half-empty pesticide
canisters. What drunken, feebleminded architect
cut a plea bargain to escape punishment for
the poor humor that is Mia's internal structure?
From the exterior she could be a model, but
like model houses the interior was never
intended for use. Her museum of pain is
tucked away in the basement, below
the maternity ward, each millimeter an
exploration of musculoskeletal frailty.

Each caress along her surface dislodges
another section of her plumbing, and another,
until stagnant fluids spill out. She keeps a bucket
at the bedside for this eventuality. A few
convulsions later she collapses onto her back,
wipes at her mouth without care, breathes: "Don't
…stop…don't…stop…" And the sperm donors
continue. If she forgets to breath through her
mouth, allows their scent to invade her nostrils,
the next round of convulsions will begin

instantly rather than being put off for a few
minutes more. The arching of her back
grimacing eyelids grinding teeth developing stress
fissures claws tearing through sheets uncontrolled
tremors is mistaken for an Adult Video
Award-winning orgasm of the year.
    Every male: "Damn I'm good today, baby, you know it…" The men
will never be hired as interpreters.
If Mia can summon the strength she lays face
down, imitating a corpse discarded in an
alleyway, hoping to conceal the dry heaves
once her stomach hangs its vacancy sign. The sudden,
shooting pains contort her body at random, five
minutes between, an hour between, sometimes
half a day before the next strikes. And each
moment the men cultivate her agony: *Please this
time please let it happen this time please pregnant
PLEASE fuckin' PLEASE god DAMNIT it has to
be over OVER please*. The unwashed hobo
squatting under her decaying maternity ward
traps the curious, those who cannot read
posted Condemned Structure signs, kills any
who might stay. The foundation sinks, slowly,
dislodging bricks in the once-beautiful façade.
BABY IS THE CURE BABY IS THE CURE

With alarming clarity the clock that is their
relationship slows, first the hour hand dying,
then the minute, both demises capable of being
ignored. The second hand weakens, and then
the spring coil is undone. Nothing binds the man
and woman together beyond a mutual desire
to serve their own needs. That, and the child
who lingers like last month's malady, one
previously believed to have been vanquished
by syringes full of cure.

Jermane: "I don't think having you around creates a safe environment for my child."
Mia: "Mouse needs to sleep. We can talk later."
She cradles the darling, frail thing in her arms, forces air over her vocal cords…

Hum-a-bum! buzz! buzz!
   Hum-a-bum buzz!
As I went over Tipple-tine
   I met a flock of swine;

Some yellow nacked, some yellow backed!
   They were the very bonniest swine
   That e'er went over Tipple-tine

The vitality seeps from Mouse's flesh. Her limbs flop as if inanimate when Mia places her in the crib. Jermane is at the ready, anxious to run her reasoning to ground. What possible excuse could she have for her past behavior? To explain that childbearing is considered the cure for dysmenorrhea, that giving birth would rip the agony still alive and screaming from her flesh, fling it to a far dark corner never to invade her tissue again, well, that would let on what is really happening with her. Would scare him away. Her brain skids along the Autobahn losing sacreal meninges and spinal fluid before hitting the exit ramp to believability…just as the bee harvests the male reproductive portion of flowers so, too, did she collect male seed for future consumption.
Mia: "The Book of Mormon, ancient Far East texts, the Talmud and Koran and Bible, they all hype up bee pollen!"
    Jermane: "Bee pollen, Mia, bee pollen. You know the difference between people and bees?"
Mia: "Yeah…bees are better, than you at least!"

The apartment is torn apart by the emotional spasms that follow.

The cornflower is withered away to a veil of blackened rot draped over the canopy of trees. It is barely a box with air-holes hastily poked through by blunt scissors in the hands of an indecent child. The graves have been robbed of their sweet morsels. Every virtue smolders, filling the narrow confines with smoke, slowly, slowly, with the unstoppable certitude of a juggernaut. Supplications howl through burnt-out pillars, empty as the gust of a death-rattle. There is no world without end as there is no end without a world.

Wide open spaces sow in Mia's mind the kind
of agony dysmenorrhea relays through her body.
Her hatred for the out-of-doors is typically only
overcome by a need to gather intelligence.
Today, though, she has run out of bee pollen,
and her mail order pharmacy service proves
hapless and heedless. Thankfully it is not the week
before her menstruation's onset or, even worse,
during her flow, because even artificial light is
impossible to endure through those shattered
weeks, much less the actual sun's full onslaught.
On the way to the store there is only one random
lightning bolt of agony, this one running through
her right side. Its aftermath brands her joints
with lingering heat, her skin with the sensation
of freon exposure. This happens occasionally,
not optimal but preferable to the weeks-long
version. In the pharmacy itself she never bothers
with the bee pollen purchase, as she spies a bloated
young w/oman conversing with the pharmacist.
This vessel is forty weeks along and the doctors are
pushing for caesarean section, but given the gaping
chasm of risk to the mother, and the exponentially
increased chance of substance abuse in the child
if the regular cocktail of birthing drugs is

administered…well, she just cannot do that to her
child. Mia's smile is that of stockbrokers noting
a national spike in cancer diagnoses. Although
it runs at odds with established protocols
Mia follows her, leading to…

Jermane arrives home from work to find
dinner ready; much to his surprise Mia is
the culprit. He thought they were through
after their cataclysmic fight, and that the neighbor's
girl was supposed to be watching Mouse. These
thoughts are cut short by the sight of the dining
room table. A crystal bowl overflowing with
decorative gourds and autumn foliage dominates
the center, ensconced by silver chargers
with matching plates on them, crowned by
fanned napkins. The good silverware left by his
Grammy Evans flanks the plates. With even greater
bafflement he discovers the waiting bottle of Dom
Pérignon Rosé. He takes note of Mia's bloody
apron, imprinted with a pseudo hand-scrawled
"the" rammed between "French" and Chef."
Mia: "Have a seat."
    Jermane: "What is this?"
Mia: "It's a special meal. Czarnina. It's a kind of Polish duck soup. I had to improvise a little."
    Jermane: "I like me some make-up food, mm-hmm. Nice and…hmm. What's that taste? It's good, not sayin' that, just different is all."
Mia: "The base for the broth is blood."
    Jermane: "Blood?"
Mia: "And vinegar, to keep it from clotting."
    Jermane: "Aw, babe, that's enough of that. C'mon."
Mia: "You'd be surprised how hard it is to come across two cups of blood."
    Jermane: "What'd you end up using, anyway? It's sure not duck."
Mia: "They call it 'hairless goat.'"
Realizing his daughter does not accompany

them at the table Jermane inquires as to her
whereabouts. Mia sets a mirror across from
Jermane to serve as his dinner companion.
His reflection is the flavor of something
parasitic, watching his mouth eating his mouth
eating his mouth eating his mouth eating. Jermane
served on a mirror makes poor company, crossing
Mia. Something about all this strikes him as improper,
but his thoughts are a little fuzzy. And the food is delicious.
Mia: "Maybe a lullaby would be nice. I'll do the same one I sang Mouse earlier."

Buzz, quoth the blue fly;
    Hum quoth the bee;
Buzz and hum they cry,
    And so do we!

In his ear, in his nose,
    Thus do you see;
He ate the doormouse,
    Else it was thee.

The meat, in light of Mouse's empty seat, is
indeed less alien now that Mia sings. But
inexplicable petrification pierces Jermane's limbs,
dwarfing cannifilicidal fears with mounting consternation.
    Jermane thinking to himself: *Is this a heart attack? This what it feels like?*
The muscle relaxants have taken effect. Mia sets
down her utensils, dabs at her lips with a napkin.
From the kitchen she retrieves her
well-used bone saw.
Mia: "The most wonderful thing happened today. I found another baby donor. I don't need you any more, and you made it clear you don't need me, so…"
If one's intent is to butcher the flesh of another

it is best to use unexpected blows to stun
the food source, or a bullet to the head, otherwise
adrenaline and increased heart rate render
the work ahead problematic. Mia has no desire
to allow him into her mouth ever again. Tears
overcome the flood walls of his eyelids, surge
over the flood plains of his cheeks as the circular
saw blade is pressed against his forehead.
Mia: "You could've been the one. Now you're just *another* one."
It is easy to tell herself that with this new
death her heart is missing in action but the truth
is her mind and very soul are missing in action.
Mouse and Jermane remain where they are as
she leaves, because "it will make a statement."

Mia draws close to her secret lair. The gabled
roof intrudes progressively into the vista's
flesh, piercing the blue diaphragm overhead,
deflating the lungs of existence until the house
looms over her, a decaying underworld blotting
out all else. The cracked slate scales of the roof
would surely slip free to decapitate her, their
iron pinnings long ago rusted to uselessness,
save for the cage provided by its balustraded
parapet. Her feet know all too well the safest
path across the sharply jutting porch; the familiarity
of her fingers with the lock are as a ballerina's
feet skimming across the floor of a dance studio.
The behemothic ruin exhales its mephitic
atmosphere with all the portentous intensity
of a death rattle, but this structure is far
from collapsing…Mia has seen to that. She has
reinforced its bones during long hours of
rehabilitation, her crude work somewhat less
pleasant than a barbed wire corset, but it holds
everything in place. When her operating/culinary

equipment is at rest once more she scans
the horizon from the widow's roost, glad to remove
the respirator required inside the home's moldering
confines. A child's jacket, tattered and bloody,
dangles from the razor wire fencing surrounding
this blasted, barren patch of earth. Her closest
living neighbors are the factories assailing
the hundred-acre property on three sides. Lurking
at police auctions has its advantages when purchasing
a second residence. Her gas-powered generator
roars from the backyard, reminding her that time
continues passing through her fingers as if it
were happiness, stability, satisfaction.

The vessel waits below, underground, in
the structure's one immaculately clean room.
Great leaps have been made in devising humane
restraints: the locking leather six point
restraint system displaced only seven hundred
dollars of her funds, yet does the work of three
attendants by maintaining an unrelenting grip
on the vessel's ankles, wrists, lower chest,
and knees. W/omen such as this latest catch have
not earned the right to scream or even cry; having
their bellies slit once is laughable in comparison
to the sensation of having one's abdomen carved
day and night for half of your existence. Their
attempts to assert ownership of such pain is an insult
so unwarrantable that murder can be the only
proper response. The vivisectionist within Mia stirs
to life, this time to paint its mural of agony on
the temple of another diety, an innocent god ripe
with unfamiliar divinity. Stainless steel glimmers
under the worklights: angular arms and blunt
prongs of the contoured abdominal retractor,
the titanium bulldog clamps, vicious ring cutter,

German carbon steel scalpel blades in the hundreds,
offset by the blue reusable surgical gown tied at
the neck and midback covered by an evergreen
heavyknit vinyl butcher's smock, the hemostatic
sponges, the baby blankets. The strands
of blackness issuing from her scalp are covered
by a translucent surgical cap and bound in a long
tail trailing between her shoulder blades.
The w/oman distastefully passes out from the metal
tipped invasion; Mia's own blackouts are also
associated with penetration, although it is by
men, and when she wakes they continue to reside
within her pain, as will the knife within this w/oman.

Boy or girl it shall be Kelly, to whom she will
bequeath undying devotion and attention, and
the very house in which he/she is born, gargantuan
as it is it can afford Kelly the space to grow
into whatever variety of adult he/she chooses,
taking however many mates might please
the heart and raising a multitude of grandchildren
for Mia to cherish, to direct in how to remove
the wicked blood of the iniquitous from earth's
stained face. This vessel herself remains nameless,
unlike so many of the others; Mia's personal
attention is usually required in cultivating
circumstances to the point of bearing fruit.
The Caesarian courses absorbed via the InterWeb,
the CPR certification, all the long hours of
training have been put to the test time and again
using social networking sites to befriend pregnant
w/omen, arranging exchanges of baby carriers,
breast pumps, cloth diapers, or anything else
the w/omen want to hear.
Little Kelly does not survive Mia's attentions.
Even an expert would be hard pressed to

anticipate the entire spectrum of neonatal
disorders that may present themselves while
"in the field" as they say, so who can blame
her, call her a bad mother? Although it is
disconcerting that some variety of complication
occurs every time. Perhaps this is fate whispering
bittersweet nothings in her ear, salivating on
her neck, the same "fate" Jermane had cherished.
Poor Jermane. If fate will deny her the joy
of motherhood, deny her respite from a life
of torture, then perhaps she is staring at her
curtain call. She has disappeared before, reborn
in a new geo-social structure with a new scent,
but this time there will be no miraculous revival.
The queen bee also possesses a stinger, but need
not die using it unless she so chooses. Weeks
later when a Victorian house is featured prominently
by media outlets she is unable to witness the spectacle.
The astronomical number of bones found in the cellar
is so ponderous investigators cannot determine
the number of corpses they are dealing with, although
the diminutive nature of many remains leads them
to believe they have solved the rash of baby
disappearances plaguing the tri-state area these last
three years. Old pain and new alike continue,
spreading in an ever-widening geometric pattern,
rhombic in dispersion. It is enough to finally force
the demise of Jermane Byron and his daughter
Marlene from the headlines. Another headline, already
forgotten by the time of the Victorian house discovery:

Police Credit Samaritan With Saving Girl
Monday, October 24, 2010 8:17 PM

A woman was killed this morning while saving a 3-year-old from an on-coming truck.

The accident occurred at 7:57 a.m. on Colm Station Road outside Colm Station Elementary School, News 7's Valerie Avon reported.

The police have verified that a crossing guard was present, but was involved in settling a road rage incident between two families dropping off their children.

Richard Dunigan, a member of the park police service, was dropping off his daughter at the regional park police daycare facility adjacent to Colm Station Elementary.

"I felt it was necessary to help that [crossing] guard restrain one of them road rage folks," he said. "That's when I lost track of my little girl."

Witnesses say Hana Miura, 28, had her arms around Dunigan's daughter and attempted to run to safety, but instead became a human shield. The girl escaped with minor abrasions.

The truck driver suffered a concussion after slamming on his brakes. When it was discovered his seatbelt was not engaged both he and his trucking company received fines. Investigators failed to uncover any evidence of criminal wrongdoing on the driver's behalf.

After notifying Ms. Miura's next of kin the authorities made another discovery.

"Ms. Miura had a history of mental illness in her youth," said Coleen Watts, police spokesperson. "Apparently she was living here under an assumed name."

Authorities in other jurisdictions have yet to respond to media outlets as to whether or not Ms. Miura is a suspect in ongoing investigations.

"Whatever problems she had in her past, she died a hero," Watts said.

*Nursery rhymes from The Nursery Rhymes of England, *1843*

Suicide, Suicide

When you're walking down the street
and you see dangling feet
Suicide
Suicide

When you're laying in bed
with a gun to your head
Suicide
Suicide

When they need a stomach pump
just to save your rump
Suicide
Suicide

You've already died
and hell opens wide
Suicide
Suicide

It's bloody, it's runny
and it's really not funny
Suicide
Suicide

It's not at all appropriate
but I went ahead and wrote it
SUICIDE
SUICIDE
SUICIDE
SUICIDE
SUICIDE
SUICIDE

SUICIDE
SUICIDE
SUICIDE
SUICIDE
SUICIDE
SUICIDE
SUICIDE
SUICIDE
SUICIDE
SUICIDE
SUICIDE

Oh, how would you dare?
Because nobody cares
About suicide
About suicide
About you
About you
About me
About me

Futher Reading

American Foundation for Suicide Prevention
The American Foundation for Suicide Prevention (AFSP) is the leading national not-for-profit organization exclusively dedicated to understanding and preventing suicide through research, education and advocacy, and to reaching out to people with mental disorders and those impacted by suicide.
http://www.afsp.org/

American Medical Association
Since 1847 the American Medical Association (AMA) has had one mission: to promote the art and science of medicine and the betterment of public health. Today, the core strategy used to carry out this mission is our concerted effort to help doctors help patients. We do this by uniting physicians nationwide to work on the most important professional and public health issues.
http://www.ama-assn.org/

Christian Medical Association
Christian Medical and Dental Associations exist to glorify God—by motivating, educating and equipping Christian doctors and students to serve with professional excellence as witnesses of Christ's love and compassion, and by advancing biblical principles of healthcare within the Church and to our culture.
http://www.cmda.org/wcm/

The Dougy Center
The mission of The Dougy Center is to provide support in a safe place where children, teens, young adults and their families grieving a death can share their experiences. Featuring information and support for teens by teens.
http://www.dougy.org/

Euthanasia.com

We are committed to the fundamental belief that the intentional killing of another person is wrong. We have deep sympathy for those people who are suffering.
http://www.euthanasia.com/

Euthanasia World Directory
For the rights of the terminal or hopelessly physically ill, competent adult.
www.finalexit.org

Not Deat Yet
Not Dead Yet was founded on April 27, 1996, shortly after Jack Kevorkian was acquitted in the assisted suicides of two women with non-terminal disabilities. In a 1997 Supreme Court rally, the outcry of 500 people with disabilities chanting "Not Dead Yet" was heard around the world.
http://notdeadyetnewscommentary.blogspot.com/

Right to Die
Do we own our own bodies or does the State? If we do, then we have the right to choose our own time and manner of death. If the State does, then are we just pieces of national property?
http://www.righttodie.info/

Survivors of Suicide
The Survivors of Suicide web site is an independently owned and operated web site and is in no way associated with any specific group, organization or religious affiliation. The purpose of the Survivors Of Suicide web site is to help those who have lost a loved one to suicide resolve their grief and pain in their own personal way.
http://www.survivorsofsuicide.com

The World Federation of Right To Die Societies
The World Federation, founded in 1980, consists of 44 right to die organizations from 25 countries. The Federation provides an international link for organizations working to secure or protect the rights of individuals to self-determination at the end of their lives.
http://www.worldrtd.net/

Genesis 6:7 So the LORD said, "I will wipe mankind, whom I have created, from the face of the earth—men and animals, and creatures that move along the ground, and birds of the air—for I am grieved that I have made them."

About the Author

John Edward Lawson has published eight books and over four hundred works in anthologies, magazines, and literary journals worldwide. He is a Bram Stoker Award finalist and a winner of the Fiction International Emerging Writers Competition; other nominations include the Rhysling Award, the Dwarf Stars Awards, and the Pushcart Prize. As a freelance editor he has worked for Raw Dog Screaming Press, Double Dragon Publishing, and National Lampoon among others, has edited seven anthologies, and served as editor-in-chief for *The Dream People*. He lives near Washington, DC with his wife and son.

www.ingramcontent.com/pod-product-compliance
Lightning Source LLC
Chambersburg PA
CBHW022119040426
42450CB00006B/760